OVERCOMING narcissism

A PRACTICAL GUIDE TO LIVING WITH A NARCISSIST

Jessie Lee Perez

Book Cover by Ness Lobo

1st edition 2025

ISBN 979-8-9857143-5-7 *Paperback*

979-8-9857143-6-4 *Ebook*

Contents

Benefits

The book "Overcoming Narcissism" by Jessie Lee Perez offers practical guidance for living with a narcissist. It aims to empower readers by providing them with tools and strategies to manage such relationships effectively. Key benefits include:

1. **Understanding and Overcoming**: The book is more than just a guide; it is positioned as a path to hope and a means to achieve freedom even amidst ongoing conflicts. It offers readers a deep understanding of the narcissistic cycle and guidance on how to navigate it.

2. **Community and Support**: Beyond individual reading, the book fosters a sense of community, offering insight for support members who can now better understand their struggles.

3. **New Discovery**: This book includes a previously undocumented discovery that sheds light on a novel phase of narcissism, which promises to transform approaches for clinicians and counselors interacting with narcissistic patients. This new understanding is also crucial for enhancing support mechanisms for individuals living with narcissists.

OVERCOMING NARCISSISM

Dedication

This book was written over a seven-year time span while walking in the midst of the fire.

I dedicate this book to all of those still walking in the fire.

May it give you what you need to make it through.

There is Hope
Chapter 1

Congratulations! You officially have permission to stop walking on eggshells. No matter what you do or don't do, you cannot prevent the narcissist from having bad episodes. So, you have full permission to take a big sigh of relief and begin to be you again!

You have probably heard that narcissists never change—thankfully, I have lived through proof that this is not always true.

In my thirties, I realized that a relationship in my life was not just violent and difficult, it was fueled by a hidden menace—the "monster" known as Narcissistic Personality Disorder (NPD). This is a true personality disorder, and it can hide very convincingly in public view. One day while sitting at my desk I did an online search for why someone would act like what I was experiencing from this person. I typed in something along the lines of this: "How can someone be nice and pleasant one second and a complete monster the next?" At this point I was just looking for a listening outlet . . . as I felt very isolated in this desperate place. The internet was my "listening ear" that day. But what I didn't expect is that it listened and gave me answers! I really didn't expect an actual answer. What came up, however, was a Mayo Clinic article on Narcissism (similar to the one I have referenced in the Bibliography). I read through it and was amazed. It described exactly what I had been in the midst of for years. That led me to another article that detailed some of what goes on in the head of someone with NPD.

About an hour later the person who I was dealing with in this struggle called, having an almost chipper tone in his voice, having clearly just come out of a dark cycle, which had lasted that past four days straight. Instead of being angry for what I had been put through for the past four days (one round out of countless others that just kept coming), I decided to get curious. This is where things began to change.

I used what I had just learned from the two clinical articles and asked open-ended questions about exactly what he was thinking and how he was relating to who he was over the past four days. I was careful to frame the questions specifically without leading the question, while leaving it open-ended for him to answer.

I was astounded! He answered exactly how the articles had described it. A shift had occurred—I finally knew what I was dealing with.

> The hardest enemy to fight is the one you know nothing about. – Jessie Perez

The hardest enemy to fight is the one you know nothing about. In most cases, the "enemy" is not the person but, rather, the "mindset," the "motives," or, in this case, the clinical personality disorder of NPD. Let me clarify that this does not in any way excuse the *person* from responsibility for their actions. They still need to be held accountable, but if you want to address this issue, the focus needs to be on the problem.

There is good news! As we journey through this book together, I'll share practical and effective steps to help you walk out this relationship, both with regard to how you relate to yourself, and how you relate to the narcissist. There is hope, but let's take this one step at a time.

Introduction:

I didn't start out as an expert on Narcissism. Inconveniently, I found myself fully in the midst of a narcissist's environment, however. Initially, I did not understand what I was mixed up in and it seemed to come on without warning. As I initially battled against violence, accusations, and insults, all I knew is that it hurt and the hurt didn't seem justified.

As far as my background is concerned, I took a few psychology classes in college, but it wasn't until I became a certified human temperament consultant that my understanding of people became transformational. Little did I know that my lifelong casual study of people and my certified training would be so instrumental in my own life, and flow over into the lives of others.

Through the journey of studying this condition firsthand, building a network of others also in similar relationships, and applying a scientific approach of testing, I have seen measurable progress. I sit completely gone, no. But progress has definitely been made. I talk more about what progress looks like in chapter 5.

It's through the small victories, rigorous application, and study through tremendous trials in my own life that I'm able to bring insight, practical advice, and hope to others also dealing with people with Narcissistic Personality Disorder (NPD) in their lives. There are so many books and articles about how to start the healing process once you get out of or leave a relationship with a narcissist—but what if you want to try to overcome without cutting that person away? I couldn't really find any material on that option. That's why writing this book became so important.

Understanding Narcissism

Chapter 2

The first thing to understand is that when you deal with a narcissist, that condition is not the root of the person. You are dealing with a person who has a clinical disorder: Narcissist Personality Disorder specifically— otherwise known as NPD. Much in the same way a person who is a clinical alcoholic will never fully be cured but, rather, is "recovering," so, too, is this the case for a narcissist. They can overcome, but the disorder remains with them, and it is a lifelong process of overcoming. It's not something that is one day just gone.

When I first discovered that the person I was dealing with had a clinical disorder, it was a relief for me. For the first time, I had hope. For the first time, I could begin to see this person not as an evil person who was completely unpredictable and bent on destroying me, but as a person, a human being like you and me—but with a very horrible clinical disorder. This separated the actions and words I was drowning in from the person who was delivering them.

Now that I had this understanding, I could start to look at the approach pragmatically—and that is where the game began to shift. Clearly this is not a game, but for the first time, I was able to see it through a new set of rules; I suddenly had an angle on the board I'd never had before.

As a human temperament expert, it is wired within me to understand why people do what they do and to find patterns within thought approaches and behavior. My years as a business analyst had also taught me how to ask the right kind of questions to get at challenging answers and how to organize the findings into meaningful insight. Don't worry, I won't take you through any of that process. What you need are answers and to understand how to successfully apply those answers. And that's just what I'm going to teach you.

The Story of Narcissism:

No matter what your specific circumstances maybe, you can gain a little comfort to know you aren't alone. You aren't the only person going through this. It is also extremely important to understand and remember that this is not normal or acceptable and that most relationships do not have this as a factor.

Feelings:

Sometimes it helps to just get feelings out. If you have not had an outlet as you've been battling through, I encourage you to freely write out your feelings here in this space. This is completely optional, and if there's risk of the person with NPD finding this, feel free to write out these answers on a sheet of loose-leaf paper that can be discarded. The idea here is not to keep these documented feelings, but to get them out on a path to setting you free.

What have you been called?

How does that make you feel?

Who do you wish would know or understand what you are going through?

What would be your best outcome if you had full freedom to decide the ending?

____

____

____

____

The Scenario:

While the person experiencing the personality disorder may be a family member, colleague, or teammate, the closer the relationship, the more challenging it is to walk away or to put separation between you and that person. A child, parent, or spouse is the most difficult to part with, as you have a special commitment to that relationship.

You may have spoken with or confided in people or leadership about the struggles you have in that relationship. If those people came from normal relationships without the added challenge of narcissism, the advice they likely gave you probably felt like a childlike pat on the back when what you really needed was someone to help you dig your foot out of the pit.

They say things like "every relationship has challenges" or "it's never one sided" or "here are some relationship tips for having a nice date" or any number of other good-sounding things for normal relationships.

The truth is that, yes, all relationships have challenges, but not like these ones. And it's true that problems are never one sided, in that there's always an opportunity to improve ourselves and our behavior no matter what side of a relationship we are on. But when it comes to being on the target side of a relationship with a narcissist, it is unfortunately heavily weighted to one side with regard to the daily, weekly, or monthly challenges faced in the relationship. That being said, it doesn't mean there aren't any things you can do to improve the relationship and improve your own actions and character along the way.

Improving the relationship with the hope of seeing a new story emerge is possible, but let's be honest about the expected results. There are two noticeable states of a narcissist: the state where he or she seems like a normal and likely even pleasant person, and the state when he or she has taken the poison or something and has emerged as some creature bent on destroying the very fiber of your humanity. I wish I were exaggerating, but if you are a target of this disorder, you can likely completely relate to this analogy. It's as if the moment-to-moment character of this person is attached to some elusive light switch and at any moment some invisible hand might unexpectedly hit that switch.

Researchers don't fully know what sets off a narcissist from episode to episode. Most of the sets of triggers leading to these events occur quietly within the narcissist's mind as he or she redefines reality of statements, events, interpreted intentions, or a number of other factors. The triggering event is also commonly not necessarily a current event, but sometimes a past event, possibly even a story from before the person even met you, that the person drags into his or her processing that flips the switch. Stress from an external factor seems to be a key igniter of this trigger as well, but again, that often all takes place within the mind, quietly sparking the sudden onset of outward destruction.

As we encounter these episodes, it's important to remember that no matter what the attack looks like or sounds like, the root cause is not the events, real or fabricated, but is a result of the clinical disorder that this person has. Set your mind to separate the language of the attack from the issue. They are not one and the same.

Let's talk a moment and separate out some helpful aspects of what you know so far. Feel free to write this on here, or on a separate sheet of paper.

What are some things that you like about the person with NPD (when he or she is not in the dark space)? List at least three, even if they are little things.

Things I Like

____

____

____

____

I've read all kinds of general posts and articles that mention narcissists. They often gloss over the extent of a narcissist's defining characteristics, however. Often, they reference an over-inflated ego, a sense of entitlement, and the poor treatment of others. While these are some features, these don't even scratch the surface of experiencing narcissists from the perspective of being one of their targets. They also don't really capture what goes into the thought framework of a narcissist, either.

Understanding not just the surface of how a narcissist thinks but the pattern that drives it is an essential element for taking steps toward overcoming.

General Understanding—Things to Know about People with Narcissistic Personality Disorder:

One thing to know is that people with NPD typically do not expose themselves as a narcissist to the world. They will often identify specific targets who receive the bulk of their narcissistic activities, while they may appear friendly and even likeable to the rest of the world. This hidden behavior means that people with NPD live among us more than we'd like to realize. The image they display to everyone who is not a target is half true and half fabricated—depending on which side of the "switch" the person is on at the moment. We will talk about that switch in a moment, but first let's understand a couple of misconceived ideas that I myself had at points in the experience.

Not a Victim of Circumstance:

One thing to know about people with NPD is that as much as we may want to think of them as the "victims" of what they may have gone through to make them like this, or believe they are just hiding behind insecurities, that's just not the case. We all have struggles in life and we all have insecurities, but that does not make us all narcissists, and that is not the true root here.

Not Rooted in Insecurity:

This was one of the biggest eye openers for me. I thought, *If I could just help him get over his insecurities, he would be nicer to me.* The problem with that thinking and approach is that it actually feeds the narcissist exactly what he or she wants in order to continue the behavior. The narcissist behavior is not rooted in insecurity(though many studies connect the two). I have found that it's rooted in a sense of over-engineered pride. That doesn't mean they don't have insecurities (of course they do), but an effort to shore up insecurities will not remove or overcome the disorder. They feel as if they are entitled to whichever status, position of power, attention, or whatever else it is that they are seeking. They will continue to break down others in an attempt to elevate their own sense of themselves.

There are studies that break narcissists into two groups, labeling the true narcissist as the "vulnerable narcissist" and the other as the "grandiose narcissist."

One article in *Psychology Today* states that vulnerable narcissists try to elevate their status to cover up for insecurity. "Vulnerable narcissists may be the true narcissists, whereas grandiose narcissists are more like psychopaths, according to the study"(Greenburg, 2021).

While narcissists indeed may try to "elevate their status to mask insecurity" (2012), the insecurity is not the root, else efforts to fulfill the insecure void would exhibit a positive trend of results, but from reviewing research, the opposite is realized.

Insecurity is unmet expectations about yourself. You could think of this as a void in your own self-realization. This could be related to the idea of stress, which I wrote about in my book *Color By Design: Why You Do What You Do.* Stress is often the expression induced when needs are not being met. With stress, one cannot overcome stress by fighting the stress. The solution to stress is to identify what needs are not being met, and to address the needs. Then the stress goes away.

Through my experience studying narcissism, and general observations of people and their self-expectations, I have learned that insecurity is not overcome primarily by addressing the insecurity. The insecurity is a symptom of the persons' mindset about themselves.

The narcissist's mindset about himself or herself seems to be the root of his or her narcissistic tendencies more so than any insecurities that he or she is perceived to have.

Grandiose NPD, as mentioned from the previously referenced article, seems to be the most popularized concept of narcissism and a focus of many mainstream interpretations of the term "narcissist." This interpretation becomes challenging for people who are encountering true narcissism as discussed throughout this book—as there is a commonly held idea that you can "spot" a narcissist, when most victims or targets of narcissistic attacks suffer silently in secret with a person who puts on a pleasant face in many public environments. To avoid any confusion with the popularized definition of narcissism, Grandiose Narcissism will not be further referenced in this book.

Through my indirect study of others caught in similar relationships, I have also encountered what I've termed "Alcohol-induced NPD." To clarify, I do not see Alcohol-induced NPD as any different from NPD discussed throughout this book, only that the most prevalent symptoms are experienced while the person is under the influence of alcohol, and less frequently or commonly when the person abstains from alcohol.

If you happen to deal with an alcohol-induced narcissist, then the narcissist may present heightened narcissistic symptoms when under the influence, while rarely showing the most impactful symptoms when alcohol is not a factor. While this was not a factor in my own relationship, it was present in at least one of the additional relationships I indirectly observed during this study. The alcohol-induced case doesn't mean the person does not suffer from NPD, but that while fully sober the person is better able to regulate and stay in the light phases.

This also means that it may be more challenging for these people to acknowledge their wrongs—as alcohol-induced symptoms may also come with a lack of memory of events and words spoken (not simply as a denial of them), akin to the memory blackout or distortion that commonly occurs as a result of excessive alcohol consumption. Recording or otherwise documenting what is said during those times can aid in use during the learning phase, which we will discuss shortly.

The Cycle

Most descriptions of NPD recognize two distinct phases, similar to Dr. Jekyll and Mr. Hyde. The first part is the light phase. This is where the person could be quite a delightful person. Then there is the dark phase. When triggered, this phase kicks in immediately and without warning. It is as if someone flipped a light switch. Then after sometime, the switch flips again into what seems like the light phase. I want to challenge this visual of a switch flipping back and forth, however . . . not that there isn't a "switch" of sorts—which I will actually discuss further in just a moment—but I want to visualize this pattern more as a circular cycle.

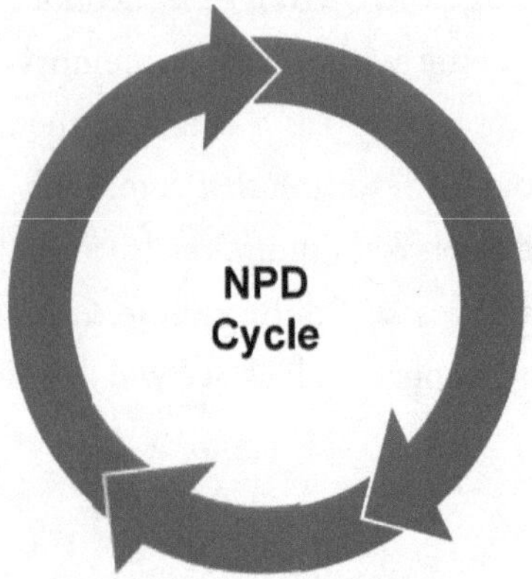

Image 1: Created by Jessie Lee Perez for Overcoming Narcissism

As I studied this condition firsthand I began to notice a slight inconsistency with the first portion of the "light" phase as compared to the rest of the light phase. I started to explore that inconsistency and out of that exploration I made a discovery that fundamentally transformed my approach to combatting the NPD condition.

Remember, the way to making progress starts by clearly identifying the problem. I had a new piece of the puzzle and the problem definition was becoming clearer.

That discovery is what I have called "the learning phase." This is the phase that a person with NPD enters upon leaving the dark phase, prior to actually entering the light phase—and it is the only phase where progress can be made. I have searched through multiple writings and articles on NPD and have spoken with several licensed professionals in the field of personality disorders, and I could not find any knowledge of the existence of this third phase. I invite psychologists, counselors, and researchers to take this finding and further study it, in hopes of bringing greater value and successful treatment opportunities for this condition to the clinical community. Let's explore this phase more as we look at the full cycle.

The cycle of NPD consists of three parts, and they are always in the same order. You can start in whichever phase you'd like as it is cyclical, so I'll start in the Light Phase.

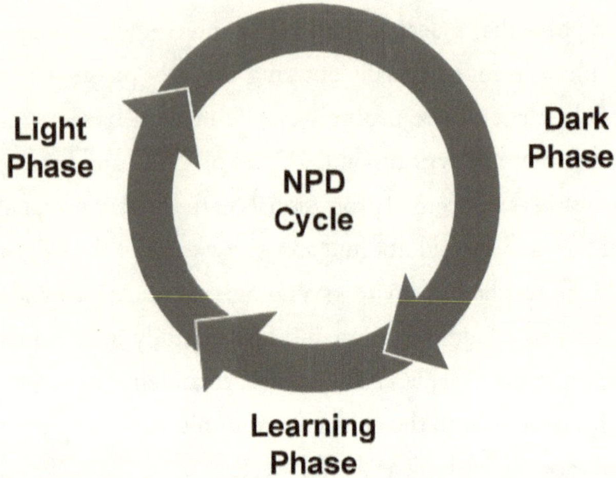

Image 2: Created by Jessie Lee Perez for Overcoming Narcissism

If you were to string these cycles together in a more real-life model, it might look more like the following, where the Learning Phase drives the person with NPD into the beginning of the next cycle. While the learning phase is the driver, remember, it is a very short time window, so any work that is going to happen must be pursued as soon as the person enters that phase. What is done in the learning Phase will impact the next phase potentially and the long-term trend.

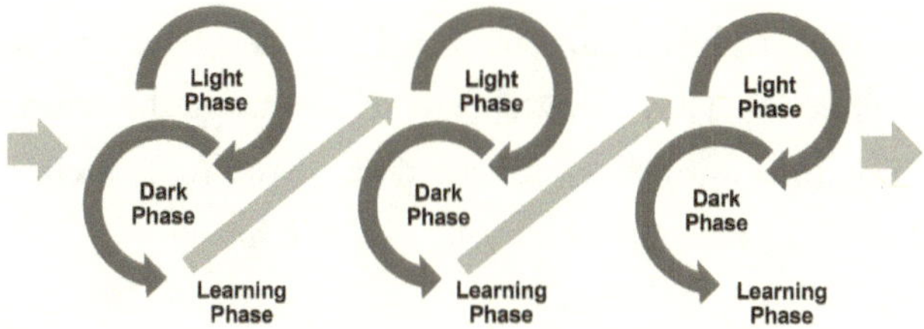

Image 3: Created for Overcoming Narcissism by Jessie Lee Perez

Contrasting the Light and Dark Phases

While in the Light Phase, people with NPD may sometimes seem pleasant, maybe initially even wonderful (or at least enjoyable).

But other times, when they are in the Dark Phase, they can seem like the worst persons you've ever met, and you can't imagine how a person could be so cruel.

It would be logical to assume that one of these states is fabricated—that there is no way a single person could be so far to the extremes of treating another human being so terribly and mean it. However difficult it is to make sense of, the person actually does fully mean the actions he (or she) is exhibiting at any given time (on either side of the spectrum), maybe just not a little while afterwards.

It is also interesting to know that narcissists are aware that what they are doing is wrong when they attack their victims, even though it may appear they are unaware. However, they are unable to integrate that knowledge into the scenario, as they are so tightly bound to denial and fault seeking during dark episodes. They aren't able to acknowledge the wrong of their actions until they exit the dark phase. And often, that acknowledgement is not actually tied to remorse.

Unfortunately, logic as we know it is nearly irrelevant when working with a person with NPD. They do not behave logically, and they cannot compute their own inconsistencies (most of the time).

When they seem kind and enjoyable, they actually .are, and they mean it. However, once triggered and they drop off into the dark zone, the person who was kind and enjoyable does not exist there. Itis the same person. They don't believe they are a different person, however; for a person with NPD, the emotions of love and hate can't be expressed at the same time in any configuration or level. The person can exhibit either love or hate, but his or her common expression of anger with the ability to remember that he or she still loves the person with whom he or she is angry simply does not exist for a person with NPD.

It is important (and difficult) to remember that when a person with NPD attacks, that attack is not launched due to some logical current circumstance that can be tracked. In other words, this person is not mad at you because "xyz" thing just happened. While an event or conversation point may have been a trigger, the attack is never about that specifically, regardless of how it starts.

The Learning Phase

The "Learning Phase" is the phase a person with NPD enters upon leaving the dark phase. This is the only phase in which a person with NPD can be reached at the logical level to promote awareness, acknowledgement, growth, and prevention. This is a short phase before cycling into the light phase, at which point the person perceives everything as "good"; and the opportunity for growth has closed. Progress can be made, however, in this learning phase and ground can be gained during this phase that can last and can be built upon. While there are somedays that may feel like one step forward with two steps back, effective guidance can make a lasting and growing difference in the cycle length and frequency of phases, as well as the growing ability of the person with NPD to catch him- or herself dropping into the dark phase and pull out before he or she gets there.

Making intentional use of the learning phase is absolutely key to progress in the positive direction. These learning phases could last anywhere from a few hours to a few days. The person will cutoff or dismiss any discussion of steps or growth once he or she enters the light phase. At that point there is no further window but, rather, a time to enjoy the break and memories of good times until the cycle comes back around again.

Even with progress, however, once a person hits the dark phase of the cycle, the attacks may feel like no progress has been made at all. The severity of that phase rarely lightens. While working through the process, the aim is to alleviate the drop into the dark phase so that the person can employ methods for handling negative emotions without dropping into that state.

Phase Duration

If you've been close to someone with NPD for a while, you've likely learned their common duration for a dark phase, and possibly for a light phase as well. While some people with NPD have equally split phases, some may stay in phases longer (either longer light, or longer dark),and often there is a progression one way or another depending on responses by the target. It is also important to point out that people with NPD do not treat everyone the same. They could seem much more moderate to those outside their target group (or individual) even when in the midst of a dark phase. I've personally seen dark phases last for nearly four weeks of continuous attacks before breaking, with a light phase lasting only days before falling back into a dark phase again. There are also cases when light phases outlast dark phases with only flashes of symptoms at times.

When the switch flips back to the light side, it literally can happen in an instant. One second, the person is calling you a horrendous name (and name calling is very common in the dark phase), and a moment later the person is asking you if you want butter on your toast, as if nothing happened at all.

Approaching these phases from the understanding that this is a clinical disorder, and not a logically approached set of emotions, is a key factor in being able to separate the person from the behavior. This is important both for your own state of health and wellness (or your journey toward wellness), and the potential to be a guide for improvement for the person with NPD.

As I mentioned, the Narcissist Personality Disorder may be thought of in a similar manner as those who struggle with alcohol addiction—a person can be in recovery (overcome temptations to succumb), but will never be fully cured. It will always be an intentional process. Also, similar to those suffering from alcohol addiction, there is no medicinal resolution for NPD; this means there is no prescription that can help. The most widely recognized form of help is talk therapy(Restivo, 2024). It is rare that anyone with NPD would actually seek or submit to talk therapy sessions, however, since doing so would require that they admit they have a problem, and that (by the very nature of what NPD entails) is not something people who suffer with it are willing to consider (usually).I say usually, as there is one sliver of the cycle when a person with NPD could be willing to admit they might have a problem and be open to addressing it.

This is a new phase in the cycle that I observed, tested, and thus, will say "discovered" as it is fundamental to creating NPD improvement, and I have been unable to find any reference to it in any existing documentation.

The Emotional Switch

Let's dive into the switch now. This will take you deeper into what is going on in the mind of the narcissist and help you better prepare for how to address your interaction with that person.

It is referenced in some form or another in many articles, and I myself have witnessed that people with NPD seem to have an inability to process emotion concurrently like most people can.

Specifically, they are unable to experience love and hate at the same time (1) a psychological phenomenon known as "splitting" (American Psychiatric Association, 2013, p. 663), it is either fully one or fully the other at any given time. This is partially the underlying element that makes it appear as if someone just flipped a switch and is completely in the "dark zone" (I made up this term when needing language to express this phase), only to switch it back . . . with the person seeming normal (like nothing just happened). I've used the term "light phase" for the latter, though it may not be so "light" after all.

They also cannot understand the range between "perfect" and "defective."

When a person with NPD sees someone else, while part of that person may acknowledge that people aren't perfect, inside his or her mind, everyone is seen as either perfect or defective—with nothing in between. The same person can be perceived by the narcissist as perfect in one minute and defective in the next minute.

This coincides with the Phases of the narcissistic cycle I have observed during my study and explained previously.

Activity

This activity will help you recognize transition points in the cycle where you can prepare to take action.

What are noticeable actions or things that happen that suggest that a switch from good to bad has happened? (Is there a certain type of silence, a particular sigh, a type of question [not including the actual attack], a certain look?) This will help you identify an oncoming switch as we go along.

Noticeable Demeanor Suggesting a Switch from Good to Bad (before an attack):

____

____

____

____

What are noticeable signs that the person has come out of a dark space back into a regular person's character? Write those here.

Signs the Dark Phase Has Ended:

This process is a journey, so as you discover clearer answers to these questions, feel free to come back and add on to what you originally wrote.

Predictable, Not Logical

Another thing to know about people with NPD is that they are predictable. They go through this cycle of stages, and it will always be in the same order, though duration in each phase could fluctuate.

There are many articles that detail common behaviors that a person with NPD will exhibit. These are typically the behaviors you'll notice during the dark phase.

"People with narcissistic personality disorder may be generally unhappy and disappointed when they're not given the special favors or admiration they believe they deserve" (Mayo Clinic, 2017).This is just one example of many.

With each narcissist, regardless of whether the person is a male or female, he or she exhibits a need to feel important or elevated. This isn't the same kind of need that the average person has, as we all want to feel valued and important in different ways. The basis of the latter is just a natural piece of humanity.

But when speaking of this in narcissistic terms, the person with NPD has a need to feel important to the extent that if they do not feel recognized as fully capable or elevated, they enter into the dark space with bitterness and spite, and they are ready to attack. They will often reverse blame, which is a very common activity for narcissists—to put the blame on the person not making them feel important. The narcissist will then try to sell the other person's words and/or actions (or lack thereof) as an attack on the narcissist, even though there may be no basis for that offense.

Part of a commonly recurring trait within narcissists is their intense interpretation of being a victim or being offended. They can create offenses that aren't there by twisting the interpretation of what they perceive or hear in their minds, as they are always on defense for an attack.

Posing simple questions is often immediately interpreted as a personal attack, as an accusation on their integrity, ability, or other interpreted virtue—either real or imagined.

An example of this could be asking a question about something a narcissist says, wherein the narcissist interprets that he or she is being accused of lying simply as a result of the question.

The irony of it is that they are actually the ones attacking, yet they are completely blind to that unless they are in the "learning phase." Their immediate response to feeling attacked is to attack the person whom they interpret as having attacked them.

During my study of one person with NPD, while the narcissist was in a learning phase, I discussed this attack-the-questioner response, asking the narcissist what was happening inside the NPD mind.

The person with NPD shared, "When I feel attacked, I feel like I have to attack."

The interpretation of a question, even an everyday question like "Do you know where the bread is?" can be quickly met with a violent outburst in response, complete with verbal attacks on personhood.

While this is a completely unreasonable response to such a question in normal conversation, any question to a person with NPD could be interpreted as an attack against them, thus triggering them to attack.

People with NPD hold themselves above others and will do whatever it takes to keep themselves in that perceived position.

Things a Narcissist Does

This section focuses on a list of activities a Narcissist does and a detailed description for each activity to help you more clearly see what you are really dealing with.

Fabricated "Truths"

For a narcissist, it doesn't matter what actually happens—they create a fabrication of their imagination and try to pass it off as truth. Then they try to convince you that their fabricated truth is your truth. While in any phase, except the learning phase, they actually believe their fake truth, so any logical or factual argument against it is completely futile. Don't waste your energy, even though you will likely face direct attacks and outright lies about events and your character.

Narcissists are only willing to acknowledge the fallacy of their fabricated "truth" when they come out of the episode and enter the Learning Phase. And that admission will only last a brief period.

Projection

In addition to false realities, "projection" is a huge device that narcissists use (accusing you of doing something that they are actually in the midst of doing, or frequently do). A summary definition of projection by Joslyn Jelinek in *Medical News Today* states, "Projection is when an individual unconsciously projects their thoughts, feelings, or behaviors onto someone else" (French, 2023).See it for what it is. Trying to call them out on their projection will likely do no good—so just notice it and understand it for what it is.

Other Attacks

Additionally, a narcissist will try to tear down anything that you try to advance in or activities for which they feel you should be responsible. As an example, it's very common for a male narcissist to trash talk and degrade the cooking of a female counterpart target (the same could occur if the male were the primary cook being targeted by a female narcissist). A narcissist with physically aggressive tendencies may even go so far as to throw out food, throw food at the target, or otherwise throw entire meals on the floor or across the room. This physical attack could be a response for the target's simply responding to the verbal attack against the food provided or the initial verbal bashing of the cook's ability.

Someone without physical tendencies may take a passive-aggressive approach and shun whatever food is prepared, by leaving to buy food out or go prepare their own food when the planned meal is presented and it's time to eat.

It's not a coincidence that food or cooking attacks are common among male narcissist actions. The intent of a narcissist is to "hit 'em where it hurts." The narcissist will attempt to target those areas that most "define" the target, whether these things are actually a defining role of the individual or just an assumed role by the narcissist. In many cultures, it is commonly believed that part of a woman's role is to prepare food for her family. Whether or not you feel that this is a woman's role—or whether those are role assignments in your life or relationship—really isn't relevant. Narcissists commonly assign stereotypical realities within their own minds, and feel that they should be served. Thus, it's highly common for a male narcissist to attack a woman's cooking, since the NPD perceives that cooking should be an inherent talent that they can disparage to inflict deeper pain.

A female narcissist may attack a male in a similar way, using the male's ability to provide. It is commonly held that the man of a relationship should be the provider, even if that's not always the way things work. Again, narcissists will lock into whatever area they think they can hit to damage a person's character the deepest—whether with socially held generalizations or personalized areas of "fault" or weakness that the target may have revealed at a previous time.

Regardless of the activities specified, the goal is control. Narcissists do not only have targets of the opposite gender but can also have same-gender targets (inside or outside their families), and unfortunately, in some cases, even their own children.

Anything that the narcissist perceives as an area of insecurity, or that generates a response when prodded, is what the narcissist will continue to use as a weapon of attack. Once it's in the narcissist's arsenal, it will always be there.

But the less the target responds to it, the less it may be used. The narcissist will always continue to use whatever gets a response. As the target overcomes the material used, the narcissist will just recycle whatever else they have in their arsenal.

It's all about control. If narcissists can evoke a response, they feel as though they are in control. If they can teardown the target's sense of self-worth, that's the level of control they truly seek. Targets have the ability to take that control away from the narcissist, however.

In the next chapter, I talk more about this in the section "Building Yourself into an Overcomer."

To best utilize your defenses, let's better understand what the goal of their control may look like.

The NPD's Goal of Control

When it comes to the types of things a narcissist does in acting true to the disorder, the primary goal is control.

There are many things a narcissist could try to control. Some common things are the following:

- Your own view of yourself;
- Your sense of reality and memory;

- Financial assets; and
- Withholding things that bring you joy.

View of Yourself

When we consider what the "view of yourself" includes, it could be many things. As human beings, we are very complex beings both inside and out. Let's look at a few of these things. You may identify other things that you would add to the list, but here are some that you need to regain or hold on to as a clear truth of who you are and not give way to the destructive accusations intended to tear you down and steal your precious identity.

Your Character

Think about this as the combination of "who you are and how you present yourself." You have likely heard of the concepts of someone being of "good character" or" bad character." When we think of someone with "good character," often words or phrases that come to mind are similar to "truthful," "stands by their word," "accountable," "modest," "humble," or other such words.

The narcissist may try to tarnish your image of your character by twisting or injecting words or actions to tear down your character and the positive things you see in yourself. No one is perfect. Even someone of generally good character has flaws. If the above words don't resonate with you, then you may find areas of improvement, and that's okay. There are a variety of other words that could be added as well. The point here is that you may have had one view of yourself prior to engaging in this relationship, or before it got so bad, and the narcissist is attempting to convince you that you are a person of "bad character." This is a bold attempt at control and one that can cut to the core if believed.

Your Generosity

You may have heard of *The Five Love Languages*. This is a book and concept that pairs very well with the temperament assessment and understanding that I write about in my book *Color By Design: Why You Do What You Do*. One of the concepts in *The Five Love Languages* is that we have different ways that we express love. And what I have discovered through my own research is that how we want to receive love is not necessarily the same way in which we naturally express love. When it comes to generosity, it is likely that your level and manner of expressing generosity is linked to your love language for expressing that you care. As you pour out your love, there is a level of generosity expressed. The narcissist may see this and target that expression as a means of control and destruction.

For example, if you give of your time to volunteer, the narcissist may say you are being "selfish" for dedicating time to "some cause" instead of caring for him or her. This is clearly a fully twisted attempt to distort reality, as the very nature of volunteering in itself is in service to others and rarely an act of selfishness. However, with such deceptive approaches, the narcissist's propaganda can almost sound convincing if you are not careful to keep the truth in front of you and stand firmly. Keeping your support network connected (even those you serve with) can help you keep your equilibrium for which way is upright in this twisted attempt at control.

Your Beauty or Strength

A narcissist will regularly attack your beauty or strength. This actually has nothing to do with how beautiful or strong you really are or how much you perceive you are. This attack is simply designed to grab something that is generally held as a treasured characteristic to have, and so words like "ugly" or "weak" are often used to devalue the concepts of beauty and strength you have. This is a generic attack but can feel so personal when faced with it in the moment.

Your Cleanliness

This is another common attack focus. This attack could be a range of concepts from your own personal hygiene, to how you keep your house, to your character. The attacks here focus on the word "dirty" in one form or another. The intent of these attacks is for them to get you to see yourself as unclean and thus unacceptable.

Your Ultimate Self-worth

A narcissist will grab whatever ammunition he or she can to strike a blow to your ability to hold your head up and see yourself as valuable. All of the above focus areas are pieces and portions of the large intent to chip away at your sense of value and self-worth. If he or she can erode your view of yourself enough for you to believe that no one else will even want you, then their level of control over you meets their intended goal and they can do as they please without the risk of you leaving—which is their biggest threat.

Realize that this is all a carefully woven fabrication and that you are precious and have a very special place in this world—one that you likely haven't even discovered yet. You are talented and lovely. These attacks are not based on logic or reality; they are deceptive meanderings grabbing at anything that will invoke a response with the express purpose of trying to tear you down and make you believe these lies.

Sense of Reality/Memory

.Narcissists will try to make you doubt your own memory of events and try to convince you to believe their "reality," which will include their denial of events and their assignment of blame.

Many have said that when trying to engage with a narcissist, they felt like maybe they were "going crazy." This of course is not the case but, rather, the effects of the narcissist's bid for control of their sense of reality.

Financial Assets

This is a very common zone of control. When the narcissist is the spouse of the target, this provides a major method by which to potentially control.

It isn't always money directly (though it often is). It could be equity portions, real estate, tax benefits (or responsibilities), refunds of any type, and the list goes on. For those living with a narcissist where finances may be a factor, this can be a major area of difficulty.

Withholding Love and Things that Bring You Joy

The greatest joy is to give love and know that you are loved in return. Thus, the most painful direct act someone can perform is to directly reject the love of another. This may be something that is used as a control method by a narcissistic parent, and it can be deeply wounding to children on the receiving end.

It can also be used by narcissistic adult children toward their parents, or even toward other siblings (I will not speak to any symptoms in youth or juveniles, as I do not have enough evidence or knowledge to explore that here). Of course, this rejection of love can also be used by a spouse, or someone else who should care for you given that person's role in your life. Sometimes this rejection can come with absolute directness through statements like, "I wish I had never met you", "marrying you ruined my life", or "I wish you would just die".

But sometimes, this rejection can be subtle yet highly damaging. Examples of this may be leveraging control over the joy of giving, or a love for holidays. For someone who shows love through giving, a narcissist may tap into your joy in giving and play on it. Destroying, belittling, and directly rejecting gifts or thoughtful gestures are examples of this.

For someone who loves holidays, a narcissist may make a point to create levels of aggressive or passive-aggressive chaos during the holiday or try to make you feel bad about wanting to celebrate or enjoy it.

There are many other examples of how narcissists may attempt to steal or withhold joy from their targets. Ultimately, however, it all comes down to methods of gaining feelings of control, superiority, and power.

The following is a real-life example of how this factor of control can unravel the health and wellbeing of what should be a wonderful relational bond—the sibling bond.

Case Example:

In this situation, a younger sister to a person with NPD was the primary target of the attacks, while the rest of the family never really saw that side of the person with NPD.

The following is a real-life story shared with me of someone who was the target of a narcissist's attacks.

"[He] verbally abuses me all the time at work. He tells me I'm a joke, my life is a joke. He says no one wants me [because] of it and that's why I will never have babies. Said that he's always liked the other two sisters and not me. Said he's never wanted me to work at the office.

"I have been dragging for a while and depressed a lot with this job. I love the office. I want to do this job. I would love to take it more seriously. [He] has been the #1 factor of me being hesitant and scared for my future [because] of the anxiety I continue to have with working with him and the way he treats me, talks to me, and my future there.

"But I am a good person that loves my family and my job and I want to continue and to succeed. I need the help and support of you all [because] I have dealt with[his] verbally abusing me my entire life.

"But he is impossible to talk to, to level with and to look in the mirror that the way he is is a problem. Everyone brushes it off and I can't. It hurts me—more than anyone realizes. I love my brother. I love all of you. But I need help with this. I literally can't handle it. It is awful.

"My mental health can't take it. The words he says to me literally make me want to crawl in a hole and die. It's that hurtful and it repeats over and over in my head. He makes me feel like my life is a huge joke and he said that no one cares about me and I'm such a loser because I'm alone. I'm fine alone, just so you all know. But I need this to change, and I need everyone's help. Because I can't take it and won't take it any longer from him. No one should be spoken to that way. And I won't deal with that from my own brother."

Anyone who has been the target of a narcissist's attack can likely relate to the above, even if the words aren't the same.

A response from an NPD person to something like that would typically be, "There are two sides to every story," and they will typically attempt to discredit the person revealing the issue, and make it sound overdramatized.

Rarely is it overdramatized . . . it really is that bad. And while there are more sides to every story, the events with a narcissistic relationship are heavily weighted to one side.

Building Yourself into an Overcomer

Chapter 3

So, what does it look like to overcome when dealing with a narcissist? Well, there are two angles to that question. The first is how *you* overcome—that is vital to coming through this whole and healthy.

The second is how the narcissist overcomes and what that looks like. This piece also delicately involves you or someone close to the narcissist, as narcissists are unlikely to make progress on their own, and someone too far removed is not often present during the narrow windows of time when progress can be made. Being able to see when a person comes out of a dark phase in the cycle is the golden element in making progress with a person with NPD.

You've probably heard a lot of people say that narcissists never change. Thankfully, I can attest that sometimes they do. There are certain activities you can pursue that could actually help in improving the phases of episodes and the behavior that characterizes NPD. I'll focus on this a lot more throughout the rest of the book.

First, I will say that I do not believe that every person with a Narcissist Personality Disorder (NPD) will come through and overcome it. Many sadly will not and those on the receiving end will need to decide whether or not to retain those ties.

For those that can or will, it is not an easy journey, and it will take the gentle, guided patience of someone other than the narcissists themselves to lead the way to better ground. This can be more than difficult for the person guiding. At times it will feel hopeless; it will be thankless (don't look for a prize or even a thank you—if you are doing it you'll need to have a personal reward to gain from the process to make it worth it), and it will take time . . . lots of time.

People need to know that they aren't alone—there is hope—and understand the practical steps they can take when dealing with a narcissist.

While this first step combination of "Refuse and Diffuse" can certainly fit into the chapter on "Practical Tactics," I am including it here, as this is an essential element in your gaining enough relief to pave the path for overcoming. You don't need to become an expert on these steps instantly, but apply them, and after a few rounds you will start to see it paying off. You can keep using these over and over.

Refuse and Diffuse

"Refuse and Diffuse." Remember that key phrase when the heat turns up in the situation. Before you respond, repeat inside your head, "refuse and diffuse."

The first part is for you to "refuse" to participate in the other person's own internal battle. This is NOT your battle.

This is a battle that the NPD person is having with him- or herself, and they would like nothing more than to drag you into it and frame you as the target.

Refuse.

Refuse and Diffuse. Remember.

The second part is for you to "diffuse"; depending on the circumstance, this could look a little different.

Sometimes you can just walk away.

Sometimes you can make a joke, a funny face, or a silly action.

Sometimes you can say that you are occupied currently, but if the person would like to talk later, he or she can let you know when a good time might be.

Sometimes, you can start singing.

Sometimes you can read aloud—anything works, even just instructions or ingredients on a box in the kitchen . . . really anything to clearly display that you are otherwise focused on something else.

Sometimes, under certain circumstances, you can say, "I understand you are stressed; let me know if you want to talk about whatever is really bothering you once you take some time."

Be cautious with this last one though, as you are opening an invitation, and the whole point of "refusing" is to close the invitation.

The rest of these can be used whenever, and should be mixed up, avoiding using the same one every time. This keeps the person with NPD not knowing what you are going to do, and unable to counter it so easily.

The last one really only makes sense when you can feel the tension rising and statements are trending the wrong direction, but you are sure that the focus is still a clear external stressor.

We will talk more about how you can effectively respond with additional detail and approaches in the "Practical Tactics" chapter.

Remember, the battle is inside the person with NPD. This is not your battle.

DIFFUSE: (Reference list: This is a great page to bookmark or dog ear.)

- Walk away.
- Make a joke, funny face, silly action.
- I'm occupied; we can talk later if you want to let me know a good time *(repeat with even-tone if necessary).*
- Start singing (it doesn't matter how well/poorly you sing).
- Read something aloud (probably NOT this book!)—pancake box, maybe?

This book is like your arsenal playbook. It's like a football coach who has a playbook for the team's strategy. One of the worst things that could happen is for that playbook to get into the hands of the other team. You have one heightened advantage here, though. Narcissists never believe they have a problem, so they would never want to read a book on overcoming narcissism in the first place. So, if they don't read it, they'll never know what's in it and the arsenal is safe. With that in mind, there's no need to leave it out on the kitchen table, but there's also no need to fully hide it. Keeping it some common place a narcissist pays little attention to is just fine.

If the narcissist does happen to find it and mentions it, shrug it off like you were just curious and it's no big deal. Even if he or she threatens to throw it away, act casually . . . like you don't really care. Whatever you do, do not give in to the desperate reaction they're seeking. If he or she does throw it away, you can always go retrieve it later when the threat is gone.

Building Yourself into an Overcomer

I mean this as nicely but as directly as I can: Stop walking on eggshells. It's exhausting to always tiptoe around trying to jump before someone says jump, avoid triggering conversations or activities, or try to preempt every little thing to avoid the attack—may I say it again?—exhausting!

Since you can't prevent dark phases from coming, stop trying. Save your energy for activities that will make a difference. In addition, when you stop worrying about triggering an episode and just start being you again, you will feel a weight lifted off your shoulders. There is so much freedom in this little step.

Before even going any further, you need to know two things. First, you are not the reason the narcissist acts the way he or she does. Second, no matter what you may have done in your life, you are valuable, and you have purpose and calling in your life. And no one, no matter what they may say, can ever take that away from you. Not even your worst mistakes *define* you.

Anyone who can look at you and call you horrendous and outrageous names and utter words to demean every part of your being, all while smiling (or not, depending on the particular person or episode) clearly does not have their head screwed on quite right.

The first thing to recognize is that true narcissism is a defined personality disorder. It has defined symptoms and patterns. It has been traced to common childhood experiences that prompt the individual to create a level of alternate reality. The person is not "crazy" and to refer to the person as such would instantly create hostility and distance with a high likelihood of instant attack.

When I use the word "attack" throughout this book, it should be interpreted in the manner in which that particular person attacks. All attacks of narcissistic nature are meant with a direct intention of creating pain and causing hurt. This hurt could be in the form of words or, with some individuals, also in the form of physical attacks (personal harm to another, property damage, or some other physical expression that would be used with the intent of [in some way] harming the personhood of another). Narcissists are highly unlikely to harm themselves . . . as they see the harm aimed at others as a form of self-preservation, as distorted and deceptive as that is.

If you or someone that depends on you for care is a target of these attacks and the attacks are physical in nature against the target, you must remove yourself or the target from the environment. This is not saying that you must cut ties if that is not your intent, but you must ensure your physical safety and the safety of those who rely on you.

This means not falling for the trap of the quick "I'm sorry" or the denial that follows. And denial will follow, sure to the standard cycle of phases involved in NPD. If you are to reenter the environment at some point, progress needs to be made, ground rules need to beset, and accountability to another person needs to be arranged. (This means someone outside of the immediate scenario needs to be made aware of the circumstances and be willing to be the accountability member. An accountability member is someone who will connect periodically with the person who acted with violence, not in a judgmental manner but, rather, as a person of influence to reinforce that people get angry, but physical response is never an option.)

Even with these things set in place, there is a real potential that the person exhibiting these behaviors will not control themselves. You must be prepared to further remove yourself or those in your care from the environment and hold that ground. Boundaries are extremely important in this process.

Outside of the context of physical attacks, there are also boundaries that need to be put in place to set you up for overcoming.

These are boundaries you can use to follow through with the next steps. These boundaries can sometimes be communicated to the person with NPD—but just know that they will cross them. You have them so that you know what to do when they do cross them.

The boundaries you need to address will be specific to your relationship and the common violations of appropriate behavior, speech, or actions you specifically experience. There are many resources online and in other books about setting boundaries. This is a study and skill unto itself. If you have not yet started setting boundaries, I encourage you to do a search on "tips for setting boundaries" and you will find a plethora of resources returned. This book will not go further into how to set boundaries but, rather, continue detailing the other important steps in your journey to overcoming.

The following steps are important for you to take to become the overcomer that you are destined to be. These do not need to be followed in order, and you can be working on multiple of these at the same time.

Enjoy the things that you enjoy.

There are things that you enjoy that you may no longer do, or maybe you still do . . . enjoy them. Recognize the joy you get from them, within reason of course. No need to go overboard, but let those things be delightful in those moments.

I enjoy great food, either that I cook myself or when I dine out occasionally. I recognize that enjoyment as it comes, and I give thanks for it.

I also enjoy a nice walk and beautiful days. I take notice of these and delight in the opportunity to experience them.

There are a number of other little things I enjoy. I make it intentional to include them in my days when possible. It makes a difference in my attitude, and it builds me up a little.

Don't disconnect.

One of the most vulnerable states in which to be is alone. Build up your relationships. If you happen to be connected with a narcissist who also has other issues, he or she may try to separate you from your friends and family. While this isn't specific to narcissism, this is a very dangerous place to be. Even if the person you are dealing with does not attempt to isolate you, you may have imposed a level of self-isolation on yourself because you either don't want to burden others or you are trying to hide the issues you are facing.

Reach out; connect with friends or family. It doesn't have to include conversations about what's going on with you and that person. Just enjoy spending time together. Do something fun together. Whatever it is that connects you best with those people, make an intentional effort to reach out and connect. The second-best thing you can have is a great support network. Don't worry about what you will say if they ask how things are going. I find it's best to be truthful, and this is how I've successfully addressed it with those who ask.

If the question is very specific about how things are going within that relationship, if I'm close with the friend or family member and I feel I can trust that person not to become a voice piece whispering it all over town, I'll share simply this: "Actually, [relationship to me] has a clinical personality disorder. It makes things really challenging at times." You may also ask them to become a support member for you. You can add something like, "I won't go into all the details or anything, but is it okay if occasionally I just let you know I'm having a difficult time, and you'll know what I mean? It's just nice to know there's someone there as support." Having a few support people is a really empowering thing.

Some of my support people know a few small details, just enough to help them understand the context of the challenges. Then this way they also aren't surprised or afraid if they hear something in the background at some point. They are just supportive.

It's important not to flood your support people with the weight of your challenges. It wouldn't be wise to reach out to them every time there's an episode, for example. These are people who are therefor you, but they probably aren't dealing with this kind of situation, and they shouldn't have to carry the weight that comes with it. They can help lift you up but not carry it for you.

Some of your support people may actually be dealing with this same issue themselves in their circle. You can support each other as well. With these support members, it's a little more acceptable to vent a few more specifics during a particularly challenging time. While I would never recommend airing all your details or talking badly about another person, when talking with someone who understands, limited sharing on an occasional basis helps each of you know you aren't alone. I am not recommending this as a common practice, but it is more acceptable than in any other kind of connection.

Here is one additional key factor to selecting your support network: As people are more susceptible to the kindness of others, it is best to select people of your own gender to avoid any misplaced feelings sure to arise due to the vulnerability experienced during trying times.

Also, enjoy the company of your support people, not just as support people, but truly endear them as friends. They can occasionally be there for you, but make sure they know you care for them just for who they are, and not just as a support. People are people; we all need to feel cared about and valued. Make sure you are intentional to find out what they are up to in their lives. Friendship always goes both ways.

If there are a few people you can trust (at work, family members, church family, etc.), approach a couple and just let them know that you are struggling in a difficult position—that your (<role of person> husband/mother/brother/etc.) is suffering from a personality disorder that is untreatable through medication; that you have times when you just need someone to know you're struggling . . . that way you don't feel so alone.

This is usually something that someone close to you would be more than willing to do. You aren't asking them to fix it. You aren't asking them to bear the weight. You are just asking them to acknowledge that there are days in this journey that will cause a real struggle for you. This opens the door for when those support members ask, "Hey, how are you?" and you can be honest some of those times to say, "I'm having a time of struggle right now" . . . and they will understand to the point that it is not a secret.

While they really won't get it unless they've been there, you don't need them to get it—you just need to know that you aren't alone and this is not a secret. Not everyone needs to know, but having a couple of individuals in different forums that you can open up to from time to time is extremely valuable in walking through this long and difficult path.

Know who you are.

Previously, I mentioned that having a support network is the second-best thing you can do. The first best thing is for you to know who you are. You may feel like you have lost yourself along the way and don't know who you are. I've heard that others have struggled with this. It may be a part of your new journey to make that self-rediscovery part of your path.

Also, it's time to put away self-guilt. This is a part of overcoming. You have likely heard all kinds of attacks against you for things you have done or haven't done—attacks designed to make you criticize yourself and your self-worth. The attacks work because the lies are often mixed in with some tiny slivers of truth. The attacker will use information that you have shared and then distort it to make you see yourself poorly. You have to rise above this. No matter what you have or have not done, forgive yourself for where you have missed the mark . . . and put away your self-guilt. You will see that when you do, you will get to the point where it doesn't really bother you when the person uses that content for an attack; you rise above it. Then you aren't sensitive to those attacks in the same way.

Finances

When possible, build up your finances or establish an investment that you could lean on if necessary. This may be easier in some relationship environments than others.

See Yourself for How You Are Really Seen.

As for getting through the dark phases, there are many tips for addressing (or not addressing) the points of attack. I will be honest, after becoming a Christian at the age of 26, I was fortunate to have had a very saturating discipleship between my schooling through Regent University and the local church with which I had membership. And because of such, I grew quickly in my understanding of the Word (Bible) and my personal relationship with God. This relationship and knowledge of the Word had been crucial in my ability to withstand the attacks that resulted from the NPD's dark phases. It is this perseverance that has brought me to a point where I can speak productively about being affected by the disorder.

When it comes to methods for making it through the dark phases as a target, regardless of the effectiveness of the methods, itis difficult. I do not want to set any false expectations, so I will just be forthcoming with that expectation. As for the methods, however, I can align these methods with just three different categories.

1. You are not alone.
2. Don't attack the attack.
3. Prepare your environment.

Methods for Overcoming in the Dark Phases

You are not alone.

Essentially, you are not alone. You are not the only person going through this. People who have not experienced this will never really understand, but you do not have to be in it alone.

When it comes to walking through this process, I don't know of anyone who could do it alone. But that doesn't mean you should put the crushing burden on someone else by disclosing all of the details to that person.

You are also not alone in another way if you have given your life to Jesus Christ through a prayer declaring you believe in Him and asking for a relationship through the forgiveness of your sin, thus opening the door to really connect personally with God. The reason this step is important—rather than just believing that there is a god—is because God is pure and He will not connect with sin. So, since everyone has committed some kind of sin (even those little half-truths, or the other bigger things in your life that you know about), we must repent of our sin and request to receive the sacrifice that was made on our behalf to redeem us and cover our past sins as if they never were. Jesus was that sacrifice. So, by inviting Him in (you can see the last page of this chapter to follow a prayer to receive Him) it will open the relationship doors to God in all His glory.

It really is quite fabulous and there is certainly no one quite like Him.

When you are connected with God, you may not always feel Him there. (I know for some people, they don't feel Him ever but, rather, only see the clear working of His hand in their lives and circumstances.) However, your relationship may grow, the more you know your Word (the actual Scriptures in the Bible, not just what a pastor/preacher/bishop says), the more you will come to know God Himself and His character. The Word itself is powerful, and even declaring from it can change the environment and supercharge your prayers. Praying words is powerful . . . but praying Scripture is super-powerful! Trust me—its effectiveness is real.

A powerful method of overcoming (just in itself) is your knowing who God says you are.

Do you know the following things about yourself? The Word says that:

- You are more than a conqueror (see Romans 8:37).
- You are fearfully and wonderfully made (see Psalm 139:14).
- You are created in God's image (see Genesis 1:27).
- You are loved unconditionally (see Romans 8:38–39).

- You are forgiven—all you have to do is ask (see Ephesians 1:7).
- You are the salt of the earth (see Matthew 5:13).
- You are the light of the world (see Matthew 5:14).
- You are free from condemnation (see Romans 8:1).

And so much more.

These are the words of God. This is what He sees in you. This is who He said you are.

No matter what you have ever thought of yourself, when you are in Christ, you are washed clean. No one—and I mean no one—can give you back the sin that Christ washed away. For someone to try to do so or put that on you is for that person to imply that God is not powerful enough to cleanse your sin, or that He is a liar. But "God is not a man, that He would lie" (Numbers 23:19a). That person who may try to hurl attacks has no power over the perfect work of God.

When you know yourself as God knows you (even if you may not see it in you) and believe it is true (for He sees beyond what you do), then your declaration of these truths not only strengthens you but often chases off the attacks.

There are several psalms that have particularly spoken to me throughout this journey. One that really stands out and seems to describe exactly what it feels like in those moments is Psalm 57.

Psalm 57 (NASB)

1 Be gracious tome, God, be gracious to me,

For my soul takes refuge in You;

And in the shadow of Your wings I will take refuge

Until destruction passes by.

2 I will cry to God Most High,

To God who accomplishes all things for me.

3 He will send from heaven and save me;

He rebukes the one who tramples upon me. Selah

God will send His favor and His truth.

4 My soul is among lions;

I must lie among those who devour,

Among sons of mankind whose teeth are spears and arrows,

And their tongue is a sharp sword.

5 Be exalted above the heavens, God;

May Your glory be above all the earth.

6 They have prepared a net for my steps;

My soul is bowed down;

They dug a pit before me;

They themselves have fallen into the midst of it. Selah

7 My heart is steadfast, God, my heart is steadfast;

I will sing, yes, I will sing praises!

8 Awake, my glory!

Awake, harp and lyre!

I will awaken the dawn.

9 I will praise You, Lord, among the peoples;

I will sing praises to You among the nations.

10 For Your goodness is great to the heavens

And Your truth to the clouds.

11 Be exalted above the heavens, God;

May Your glory be above all the earth.

I value how it ends in praise to God, as there is so much power in praise and gratitude.

Let this intent stay with you a while as you consider it and its role in your life currently. Then we will talk about additional tactics you can use to overcome in the moment of attack and along the journey.

Practical Tactics

Chapter 4

Practical Tactics—What Works and What Doesn't Work

Let's start with what doesn't work (you've probably tried some of these)—logic, arguing, compromising, submitting.

Why don't these work? Let's look at why these don't work.

Logic

Using logic does not work. To the rational mind, you may be able to apply logic and it can open doorways and carve room for mutual understanding. There is no logical bypass in the mind of a person with NPD however. No attempt to appeal to logic will make any impact or have any affect.

Arguing

Arguing is futile with a narcissist, again for similar reasons as the inability to apply logic. A meaningful argument has at least two sides . . . with each contender attempting to prove a point or win the other participant to their point of view. However, the person with NPD only sees their own intent to crush any accusations and create damage. There is no goal to win the other person over to their way of thinking, and certainly not to hear, let alone consider, the angle of the target. An argument for a narcissist is about inflicting pain, not winning an emotionally charged conversation. There is no point in attempting to argue with a narcissist.

Compromising

There is no true compromise with a narcissist except your own compromise. They may verbally agree to a compromise, but there is no intent of actually upholding that commonly shared ground. Narcissists will happily accept the compromise you make for them, but it will never be acknowledged and it will never be enough. You could give up every single thing you stand for and it would still never be enough, so decide what you will and will not give up in an attempt to make it through. There is no shared compromise in a relationship with a narcissist. Set your boundaries and continuously make them known.

Submitting

This ties in with the concept of compromising. Like with the above, it will never be enough. You will never submit enough to get the narcissist to lighten up on you. The farther down you allow that person to push you, the more he or she will continue to push. Again, decide your boundaries and reiterate them as needed.

Practical Tactics—What *Does* Help

Don't attack the attacks.

The person with NPD is looking to cause hurt. If you respond in defense to the attack, you are buying into exactly what the person is trying to create. The attacks are not based in logic. The aim of the person attacking is to grab anything that they think will cause pain or can be used to attack your character, including attacking the character of others who are close to you with loose associations—attempting to tie it back to your character. When they are in this phase, nothing is off limits for use in their minds. There is no mercy.

Do not address the attack more than once. This will be challenging—as the same attack will likely come up again and again. Aim to regulate your voice tones to not appear defensive; rather, adopt a simple matter-of-fact tone. Once you have addressed the attack initially, you can point out that you have already provided a response that the person can refer back to if necessary. You can add the advance notice that you will no longer be participating in that conversation or line of questioning. Then you must refrain from further addressing it. You will literally need to ignore the attack as if you don't hear it, or else speak aloud words of affirmation over yourself or your day. Even in this, tone is important— as an emotionally gripping declaration of affirmation could be perceived as the person's achieving his or her goal in getting to you. Even if that is true, and it usually is, work on having it not appear that way. As you become more familiar with the common attacks, they won't hurt as much and some of the dismissal will be real. They really don't know how you are receiving the attack unless you show it.

If the attacks fail to get a response, they will eventually slow and the person issuing them will leave your space.

Do not engage the attacks.

This is slightly different than the first one which was, "Do not attack the attacks." "Not engaging the attacks" is number one on the tactical list. This doesn't mean you have to completely silence yourself. Actually, you shouldn't sometimes, as that could give the attacker the impression that he or she is getting to you, which fuels the attacks. You will need to learn the balance between the image of completely ignoring (silence) and the next three tactical approaches.

So, what does it look like to not engage the attacks? Here is a real-life conversation held through text between a husband and a wife (used with permission). The husband is the one with NPD, and the wife did a very good job in not engaging the attack.

The wife received a text midday one day from her husband out of the blue, and the messages unrolled as follows:

- *Husband:* You are an envious person, that's why everything you do is not prosperous. But you have to change your way of thinking in your heart because THAT is not good, especially with your own husband.
- *Wife:* You have definitely got your perceptions misaligned. Figure out your issue buddy.
- *Husband:* For a long time I always saw that you were envious of other people. But I did not want to say until today, you are definitely an envious person.
- *Wife:* Sorry, but no. Stop watching those crazy movies. They are not helping you. Certainly not helpful for our relationship. You were doing pretty good for a little

while there.

- *Husband:* You are the person who has envy for a long time. I was thinking you're not a person like that but now I discover you are like that, that's why when you say you only fit with some groups of people, it's because you think you're higher than them and you can't fit with the other people because they are socially acceptable so you can't be higher than them, that's why.
- *Wife:* Dude, what is your deal? You're having some serious issues today. Chill out and go find some prayer time.

As you can see in this exchange, the accusations and attack didn't really seem to have logical flow but, rather, was the same attack worded multiple ways. Toward the end, when the attack wasn't getting the response the person with NPD was driving towards, an additional element was added that wasn't connected to the original accusations. This is common when the attack is not received by the target. The person with NPD will grab at whatever he or she can for additional ammunition, even if the additional parts are completely disjointed from the original.

While the wife, and recipient of the attack, was not showing kindness, recognize that this attack started with a random text midday starting with the attack "you are an envious person . . ."—and I can assure you that this was not the first round of attacks this wife had been through.

In this exchange, you can also note the wife's responses. The first thing to notice is that she did not become defensive to the attack content. It is a natural response for one to become defensive when someone has thrown an accusation at him or her. But you'll see above that she did not directly address the accusations during the engagement with anything more than a statement "sorry, but no," and this was midway through the attack. The second thing you can notice is that what she did address is the act of her husband's throwing the attack; she made it clear through her response that this was an issue occurring within him and that it was unhealthy.

Interestingly enough, she shared later that while no other communication occurred between them that day until they had both returned home from work, when he did come home, his demeanor was pleasant as if nothing had happened at all.

While this instant shift is common as I've discussed, it also means that her response to the attack earlier in the day was successful—otherwise, he would have come home still in the dark place.

Prepare your environment.

There will be times when you will need to separate yourself from the person with NPD during his or her dark phases. (This is without physical harm being a component.) There are just times when the attacks are too strong, go on too long, or you are just too weak (for whatever the reason may be) to be able to handle it. If possible, create a space that's yours that you can remove yourself to and just be you. It is advisable that this space be either a space the person would not enter for some reason, or that it have an alternative way out (if you need to further exit): a room having a second exit, or even your car could make potential options. This is not always an option, but even if all you have is a bathroom, prepare yourself a comfy blanket and pillow if you need to retreat, as it will help you take that time with relative comfort—as a single attack could persist for hours unrelentingly. Having a means to get comfortable is a help. The good news is that if you have the ability to remove yourself to a separate space and you are not responding to the attacks, this should greatly reduce the attack duration.

In addition to identifying your spaces, preparing your environment also means recognizing patterns of activity within dark phases and preparing for them in advance. This can mean recognizing patterns of triggers (and you may not get these easily or at all, if the person is more strongly introverted) that bring on the dark phase. Many times, external stimuli prompt the onset of a dark phase; it could be a simple question or even a thought to tip the person over the edge. Remember that the person being triggered into this phase was not your fault; this is part of a cycle that the person needs to come to awareness of and learn how to prevent. If you do begin to recognize triggers, this may allow you an opportunity to take the initial action of disengaging from the environment in preparation. This could mean something as simple as engaging in another activity (like picking up a book to read), or more extreme (like physically removing yourself from the shared space).

Learn to finish the sentence.

One weapon in a narcissist's arsenal (which you'll notice is actually pretty small, as they like to reuse the same things over and over in slightly different ways or combinations) is to try to tell you who you are. This is an attempt to defame your character. You, however, are in the driver's seat of your character. Does it need some work? Maybe (after all, none of us are perfect). We can all improve. Does it mean you should be insulted and degraded? Absolutely not! So, the next time the attack starts with "Do you know what you are . . . ?" answer the question. "Beautiful!"

- "Amazing!"
- "Lovely!"

The list goes on. You will want to laugh (at least internally) the first time you see the attacker's response. For the first time, you are in the driver's seat, and it is a split second of utter confusion to that person. In that moment, he or she will be caught off guard and have to pivot. That will be followed by a "no," and then the person will attempt to complete the sentence of defamation. Remember, though, that you always have permission to finish those sentences. While they may learn not to look frustrated by your responses, they most certainly are, as it is an impediment to their objective each time.

We can use the words God calls us, as written in the Bible, to speak over ourselves. I find that these offer a great list to refer back to as wonderful responses. Remember the list we started in the previous chapter?

Of course you don't have to stop at one response. If the attack continues down the path of character statements, feel free to continue to stake your claim in who you are (at least for a few). And feel free to smile, because it's true and very freeing. Remember that after a few, it is best to disengage. You don't want to give the impression that you are actually responding to the attacks or that the person has any control of when the engagement ends (or doesn't).

When you make these affirming declarations, however, you are not only taking some power back in the moment, but you are also speaking these life-affirming declarations over yourself, which is really powerful . . . and you are also planting seeds into your attacker's subconscious that may sprout and gain roots someday.

Pick your favorite happy songs.

Some people will be more comfortable than others with this one. The idea here is that you actually sing. This is a great one if the attacks come while you are doing dishes or something and you really aren't in a good position to leave the room. If the attacks begin and continue after a bit of ignoring, simply begin to sing. Sing out loud. You want to make it clear that your mind is on other things, and you are not engaging in their attack.

I love to sing worship songs and praise that I've learned from modern Christian music (fun to listen to as well), or old-time hymns or gospel music. These are great for three reasons: First, they are clearly never about the attacker. Second, if you actually have a relationship with God, you get to turn to that relationship in the moment and connect in. Lastly, whether you believe in God or not, when you sing words that come from His

Word (which most of these songs contain), there is something that happens in the atmosphere—even if ever-so-slightly—and you'll notice it even inside you at times. There's a peace that nudges.

Of course, feel free to pick whichever songs you enjoy, but singing them out loud is key. It doesn't matter how you sing. You could be a great singer or a horrible singer—it really doesn't matter; you just get into that song and the attacker will realize that the attack isn't working. Sometimes this will just cause them frustration and they'll try other things, but other times they'll quit the attack and leave the situation. Note that this does not mean that they are back on the light side and you can talk to them normally again. But, you may stop singing (if you'd like). If they start back up, just start singing again.

Take up reading.

Get yourself a few books you think you'd enjoy. As you've probably guessed by now, I highly recommend the Bible as one of them. If you've never been a reader before, I suggest getting a little more comfortable with it—it could serve you well. Your engaging in reading not only can serve as a distraction for you during the person's "bad" times, but also can work similarly to the singing approach, provided you read the material aloud (unless it's this book).

Again, I find that reading biblical materials brings extra power to the words, though really any book will work. I would say that if you want to try the biblical text, a great portion of the Word to try is the book of Psalms. The Psalms are slightly poetic in nature and there are two general themes to the Psalms that both work nicely with your circumstance. One theme is uplifting and encouraging, and the other theme is call-outs for help against those who attack us.

I will note that it is not uncommon for an attacker to create an attack based on following or having interest in or involvement with the Word of God, God Himself, or church. But even still, that's just another attempt at the same old patterns, just another weapon in his or her arsenal. But this one just happens to be a piece that will serve you in strength more than it can serve them in an attack. I don't know about you, but I'll take all the strength I can get.

Walk away.

You are probably thinking, "Yeah, I've tried that, and it doesn't work; he/she just followed me with the attacks." I know it seems like wherever you go, he or she just follows you until you are cornered. This is important to know because that is part of the person's subconscious intent. If he or she can corner you, then you are a fully attentive audience for the attack . . . or so they think.

And just because you may be able to walk away doesn't always mean you should—but it is definitely a good option to keep available. When it comes to walking away, it will become more effective as you employ some of these other tactics. Once your attacker realizes that he or she doesn't have the upper hand on you as he or she was used to having, then walking away can become an option in some instances.

Sometimes this will mean walking to another part of the house; sometimes this may mean going outside; and sometimes you may just need to take a brief drive or run to the local store to buy a juice or pack of M&Ms. For those who experience jealousy as part of the attack equation, be mindful to limit driving away to very short trips or be prepared to hear an earful upon return. I also would not advise this as your primary tactic. Really, this should be a last-resort, "take a breath" option for anyone—that is, unless you actually have somewhere to go or an errand to run (in which case, good timing).

Don't get cornered.

Ideally, don't get cornered. Rooms with more than one exit are ideal, as they provide an alternative if the other is blocked by the attacker. Also, having a central piece of furniture when you get in this situation can be very useful. Appear as if you are not cornered but slightly distracted in "doing something else." Pick up an article of clothing and fold it—or appear to be looking for something. Then when you attempt to leave, you may have led them into a position for you to pass by and exit. This is a sensitive move, because you never want to "look" like you are trying to "escape" the situation, even though that is exactly what you are doing. By looking like you are trying to escape, you feed the attacker. The exception here is if your attacker ever gets physical; in such cases, if you think that could occur, it doesn't matter if you look like you are escaping, you just get out . . . and get beyond reach—far beyond reach, if you are able to do so.

Sometimes you can't get un-cornered feasibly, in which case, employ one of the other options you have available to you. Casually pick up a book and begin to read; reading out loud isn't always necessary, but it works a lot faster and makes it less likely that the attacker will snatch the book out of your hands. Of course, if you don't have any books around, dive into your favorite song acapella, and feel free to add your favorite dance moves to it.

Ignore the attack.

This is a tactic that is the least effective of those on the list, but once you've begun to employ the others, it can be used. When an attack begins, you can choose to pretend to ignore it. You can also mix this one in with some of the others.

Essentially, if after a period of time the attacks are still coming, it's recommended to try one of the other approaches.

Ignore the pre-attack.

The pre-attack consists of those things that suggest that thoughts provoking an attack may be brewing inside the head of the person. Ignore the glare (any look that he or she may give to intimidate you). Ignore it and act as if you don't even see it. Go on about your happy business.

While ignoring the attack may not be the most effective tactic, definitely ignore the pre-attack.

Mix them up.

When using these tactical approaches, it's important to mix them up. You want the attacker to be unsure of your response. This will help you take back some of the power they think they have or strive to obtain. If you use the same approach every time, he or she will be able to predict your move and it could be interpreted that that is your "hiding" spot. It may very well be, but you don't want your attacker to know that. It's important that you keep the edge to keep him or her guessing as to your response.

Be cognizant of your wording and tone.

When they start to pick and twist words or actions to cause the fight, you can call it out:

"No. You are making things up to start a fight, and I refuse to participate. You can fight with yourself."

If they continue, no matter what is said, stand out of it. You can occasionally restate, "I'm not participating."

Your tone in these words is just as important as your refusal to engage. Let your tone be "matter of fact," like it's any regularly stated fact with no emotional interest. It doesn't matter how you may feel on the inside, just state it like you have no emotional involvement. This will usually diffuse the immediate impending attack.

It may take a few cycles before the application of these tactics works well, as the person with NPD will be so confused when you start using them that the immediate response could vary from very effective to absurdly irrational. But if you stand your ground until you can walk away—if the circumstance allows for an exit, otherwise just continue to refuse to engage—then you will see this become effective.

Some Other Important Things to Consider

Forgiveness

Forgiveness—This is going to be a key (essential) part to your being able to function within the relationship. If you don't have this or can't come to this, then it's going to be really hard for you to activate the steps necessary to make an impact during that learning cycle stage.

When it comes to forgiveness, if you have a relationship with God through Jesus Christ, then you already have a sense of understanding of what forgiveness is and how it works. If you don't have that relationship, it's a little bit more abstract to understand forgiveness because you haven't experienced it in the same way. The Bible talks about our need to forgive somebody seven times seventy times. For all the math geniuses, that's a lot. When you're dealing with a narcissist, it might be more than that.

The thing to remember that will help you bring yourself to a place where you can offer that forgiveness (and please know this is not forgiveness so that they can receive it, because usually they won't think they need it—but this is forgiveness that will set you free to continue walking out the steps that you need to take) is that you are not dealing with the evilness of a person, you are dealing with the evilness of the personality disorder. We have to be able to separate the person from the disorder in order to reconcile in our minds why we're giving forgiveness as easily as we need to be able to do for our position in the relationship. Let me preface that the person will not ask you to forgive him or her. Don't look for it, and don't expect it, because you will not get it. You need to be willing to forgive regardless of whether or not they ever apologize or have a moment of remorse.

So, how does forgiveness work?

The first part is for you to let go in your heart. The easiest way to do this is to separate the action from the person. Yes, it is the person who did the action, but it is the action you despise, not the person. If you are taking the time to read this book then you still have a level of care and hope for your relationship with that person and, thus, hold such for that person.

Forgiveness will be freeing to you when you can acknowledge the way you felt about the action and move forward—seeing the person in light of the human being about whom you care.

Forgiveness holds no record of wrongs. Will you remember it happened? Probably. But you will not hold a record of it. You won't use it and bring it back up to prove a point or pile up evidence to win a battle. You will let it go; let it live in the past as a bygone and move ahead of it.

Forgiveness can be hard, especially when someone continues to do the same unacceptable things over and over again without remorse. If you hold on to unforgiveness, however, the other person is not affected by that . . . but you lose two things. The first is your own peace and freedom to live in joy; the second is the positioning you have to assist in the process of change.

Forgiveness Does Not Equal Trust

Forgiveness—We talked about the importance of forgiveness in this process. There is a truth here that I don't want to overlook, which is that forgiveness does not directly constitute trust.

Just because you forgive someone does not mean that you can automatically trust that person again. Trust is natural only in the beginning. Children can naturally trust. But when trust is broken, a shift happens. I like to trust others unless they prove that they can't be trusted—to hope that people are truly trustworthy.

But in narcissism, when those symptoms arise, trust is broken. When someone intentionally causes another person harm—emotionally, mentally, physically, to the corruption of relationships, destruction of opportunities, lying, deception, sabotage, and more—forgiveness can be given, but trust is severed.

Even as you work through this walk toward freedom and improvement over narcissism, the factor of trust can still be a hurdle.

When that trust is broken again, it takes acts of intentionality and consistency for that trust to be rebuilt. A person with NPD often has a challenge with functioning in action and consistency over their narcissistic ways.

You, however, can give forgiveness even while still working toward hope and toward steps of trusting again if that trust is earned. When there has been a pattern of lying and destruction, trusting again can be difficult.

The truth is that even when things are going very well, another episode could arise. If it does, the work towards trust starts again. This walk is a hard journey. What's in it for you?

While a person may break your trust, be cautious not to put up walls preventing you from trusting anyone. There are plenty of trustworthy people, and your shutting yourself off from trusting anyone is not a healthy course of action. To do so would mean your closing off your heart to the beauty and goodness there is to experience.

God Himself is a place in whom we can seek hope, and in Him we can trust. He is there for us, if only we seek Him and believe. He is a constant help even in times of great turbulence. The Scriptures say, "Trust in the Lord with all you heart and do not lean on your own understanding" (Proverbs 3:5).

Understanding Yourself at the Color Level

I teach a colors methodology to help people and teams understand themselves in really clear ways. When it comes to being an overcomer, having this insight is a major tool in your toolbox.

It helps you understand where you are on the conflict meter, how you address (or resist addressing) conflict, what your strengths are, and why you do what you do.

My book *Color By Design: Why You Do What You Do, Think What You Think, Care About What You Care About* gets into this much deeper, and I highly recommend checking it out, but I want to give you some of the essentials here that will help you in this journey.

The colors used in the analogy of how we are wired to think about ourselves and the world around us are Orange, Blue, Gold, and Green. While we are all a spectrum of all four colors, each one of us has brighter and paler colors driving what we do and how we approach life.

Those with bright Orange are the adventurous, risk-tolerant types, while Blue is characterized by its need for connectedness and to be helpful. Gold is by far the most organized and structured of the colors, and Green is highlighted by the logical and big picture visionary way of thinking.

None of these colors are better than any other color, and all colors have both positive characteristics (brights) and negative characteristics (shadows). By better understanding the details behind this, you can learn how we handle situations and how to process challenging situations. As you learn more about this methodology, you can become more prepared to draw upon and cherish the innate strengths you have within you.

To learn more about this, you can get the full approach and how to apply it in my book *Color By Design: Why You Do What You Do*, available anywhere books are sold online and in several languages.

Move Forward in Progress with a Narcissist – Working the Cycle

Chapter 5

What Does Progress Look Like?

Progress will be on two fronts—yours and the narcissist's.

For you, progress is becoming solid in your worth of who you are. Becoming solid in this is so powerful. You are valuable; you have great worth. This is not based on your current ability to see it—it is inherent to who you are.

As for the narcissist, progress looks like shorter dark events and longer durations between dark events. The actual events and attacks of the dark times will not be less intense or less viscous. Unfortunately, while in the midst of it, it may not feel like any progress has been made . . . as the attack is still just as difficult to press through. However, in this journey, it is so important to look at the big picture.

Let's further explore how this progress trend may look.

Observing Results toward a Positive Trend

The word "trend" is key here. When (sometimes "if") positive progress takes place, it will be observable as a trend. Conceptually, the question is asked "how does the situation look over time?"

The reason this is so important to understand is that in the midst of a "bad time," it will often be just as severe as any other bad time, making the moment just as difficult to withstand. You must continue to remember that this is not about you, how you look, what you did in your past, how well you cook, who your family is, your personal taste in life, or any other thing that seems to be a target in your particular situation.

The subjects are reused by the attacker because at some point they evoked a response. This is not about you—this is about the disorder that this person is dealing with; this is a fight they are having inside themselves. The more you can let that fight happen inside the attacker, and resist his or her effort to get you involved, the better you will get through each of his or her episodes. Keep in mind that sometimes this means separating yourself from the immediate environment.

So, when I say "trend," the trend in a positive direction could take on two forms—and hopefully both eventually.

One is the duration of time between incidents. If you observe longer periods of time between bad times, that is a positive trend. (Keep in mind this is not the observation over a week, but rather continuous trend across months, a year and even years) - this is not a fast process.

The second is the duration of the event. If bad times used to last four days and now they're down to two days on average, that is a positive trend. Those two days may still be ridiculously brutal, but it's an indicator that there is motion in a positive direction.

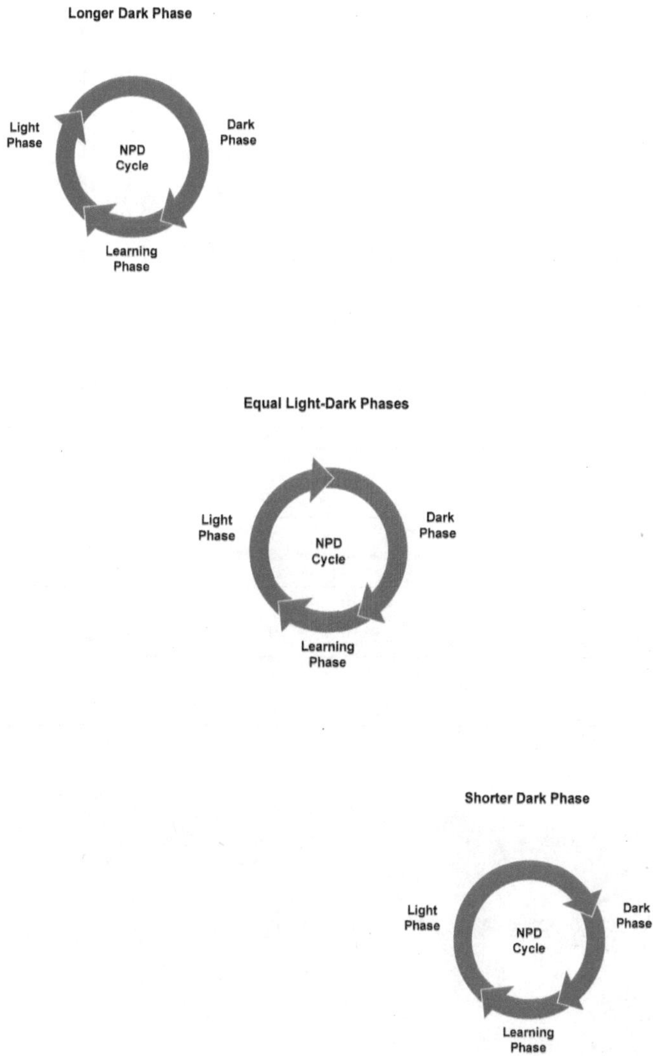

Image 4: Created by Jessie Lee Perez for Overcoming Narcissism

Use this log to gauge progress. You can use estimated percentages. It doesn't need to be exact.

Average duration of dark event (Example: 2–4 days; 3–4 weeks)

____

____

____

____

____

____

Average percentage of the year in dark events

Average time between dark events (6–7 days; 2–3 weeks; 1–2 months)

This is the amount of time from when a Dark phase ends until the next Dark phase starts on average.

As you go forward, it's going to be this type of record keeping that will help you see and remember that progress is being made. You'll never be able to judge the progress by the impact of the event—the events won't get easier. I'm sorry to have to say that, but I want you to be able to understand the reality so that you can take advantage of the progress that is being made and not discount it due to the impact of each event. Progress can be made, but you need to know what to look for.

Making progress with a narcissist takes a lot of intentional effort and can be hard to keep up continuously. Give yourself permission to take breaks. After a little progress has been made, it's encouraging to keep going. The process is a very one-sided burden—the guide's burden . . . kind of like a caregiver for the sick. You will need a break.

If you live with the person, taking a break may look like maintaining the status quo, following the steps of not engaging, but not pursuing the thankless effort of bringing transformation in the learning cycle, which often requires you to step in and be exceptionally kind, even when the narcissist has been exceptionally cruel only moments before.

Just like any effort, however, you can't stay in the break. If you want to make progress, you have to pick back up and continue with the work. You likely won't lose ground if you continue yourself-managing efforts. But to gain additional ground, you'll have to go back in during those learning phases.

How to Use the Learning Phase

How do you utilize the learning phase? The exact wording will vary, but there are certain targets at which to aim.

The objective in the Learning Phase is to move the person with NPD toward awareness, acknowledgement, growth, and prevention.

> You cannot prevent Dark Phases, but you can be a catalyst towards progress.

You can't prevent a Dark Phase from happening, but you can move the narcissist toward preventing it from happening.

Let's look at each one of these goals to understand them.

Awareness

We want to move the narcissist toward being aware of the things he or she does. The person needs to become aware that he or she has a problem.

Acknowledgement

Once the person with NPD is aware of his or her actions, ways, or mindsets, then it is time to move him or her toward acknowledging that what he or she did, said, thought, or perceived was damaging to the things that he or she may desire.

The key here is to find that personal impacting factor, or factors, that matter to the narcissist. If he or she doesn't care about you, then showing how what he or she does hurts you is not going to motivate that person to change. But, if that person wants a good relationship deep down, that could be a motivating factor if you can help show him or her how these actions, ways, or mindsets are damaging or blocking the good relationship that the person wants to have.

Finding those things that are meaningful to the narcissist is one key element. The second is to name the activity that the narcissist did that blocks him or her from having what he or she cares about. The more specific you can name it, the more likely you are to get buy-in that brings acknowledgement. Remember, this needs to happen during the Learning Phase to be effective.

You can use questions to help establish that buy-in. An example may look like this:

You: Can I ask you something? It's kind of a serious question.

Narcissist: Okay.

You: Do you remember what happened earlier today? *[or yesterday—name the time, make it recent]*

(The Narcissist will say yes or pretend not to know.)

You: You called me a lot of really bad names. I bring this up because I know you want people to look up to you at church. I'm curious if you thought about how those actions may affect the way people see you if they knew you acted like that. Is that something you considered when that happened?

Narcissist: No.

You: Do you see how maybe people wouldn't look up to you if you keep doing that?

(This is an example that you may have to work up to, and of course this may be very different than your actual example.)

Let's walk through what happened in this conversation.

First, you asked permission to "ask."

(This could look differently each time, but ultimately, you want their buy-in to even have the conversation, otherwise it could backfire or be shut down—though usually, during the Learning Phase, you are fairly safe.)

Second, you brought the narcissist back to "awareness"; are you aware this happened?

(If the person denies anything happened, he or she may have already entered the Light Phase and it's too late for the conversation to be effective.)

Third, you verbalized what happened. (Earlier on you also named when it happened.)

Fourth, you connect the reason you are bringing it up with something he or she cares about.

Fifth, you ask the person a question that will draw him or her into acknowledgement of the impact of his or her actions. Name the impact as well.

ACTIVITY

Think about the last situation you went through. If you had been able to leverage the Learning Phase, what situation, action, or mindset would you Name?

1. How would you have asked for permission to "ask"? Write how you might phrase that:

2. Using what you wrote in the top section identifying what you would have named, write what you could have said to bring that person to Awareness about the situation:

3. Combining the Named action or mindset and the thing that the narcissist cares about, write how you may have connected the action with an impact causing a consequence to that thing he or she cares about:

4. Ask them a question that will help them buy-in to how this action, mindset, etc., can be hateful to the thing the person desires. Write how you might say that here:

Growth

Growth comes out of successful engagement with the above. The more buy-in you get for the resulting consequences of their actions, the more growth they will be able to achieve.

One challenge in this area, however, is that people can typically only work on one to two changes at a time successfully. That means that while there may be thirty things you could bring up, if you do that, there will be no growth. For each Learning Phase, you will need to limit it to one or two (at the maximum) impact items that you want to bring up to address.

Then wait until the next Learning Phase comes around to go deeper in that one, or focus on a new one.

Prevention

Prevention comes with a goal out of buy-in. Ultimately, you would want to work toward a buy-in that helps the narcissist see the value of becoming aware that he or she is going to drop into the Dark Phase, be bought into the consequences to that which can damage what he or she wants, and then self-regulate to prevent himself or herself from dropping into the Dark Phase in the first place.

Getting to this place is a very long journey (if you ever get there at all), but each step is a step toward this. Each acknowledgement brings the narcissist one step closer to realizing consequences and being responsible for his or her actions.

These steps are how to leverage the Learning Phase for progress. The more you are able to use the Learning Phase to edge a little further into progress, the better. This is a lot of work, however, and there may be times when you just don't have the energy. That's okay. The cycle will come back around, so you can catch the next one.

However, if you choose to do nothing, then nothing will change. The narcissist will not change by his or her own accord. Narcissists need a lead to help walk them through that process. They simply don't have the ability to do it on their own.

If you are married to the person who has NPD, then you likely have something that you enjoy about that person when he (or she) is in the "good times," otherwise you probably would not have married the person in the first place. Depending on the level and state of the NPD, you may fight to remember the things or ways that you enjoy, especially if the good times are few and far between. I've had times when the person I was dealing with had bad times that went on for nearly four months with barely a break. It's in those times that you think you might break . . . but hold on to you—don't get lost, don't give yourself away. Find yourself in God. I don't say this from a religious view, but from the truth of what knowing yourself through God actually brings.

He tells you who you are. So, no matter what the person with NPD may say, you have the truth to which to cling. Second, the battle to forgive "seven times seventy" seems impossible and it is so easy to hold anger and bitterness toward this person (and rightfully so)—but to hold such not only binds you in anger, but also puts a wall up against forward progress and a path out of narcissism.

So, remember those things that you like about the person in the good times. Also, try to find the good things quickly to make the most of them.

Here is one additional point: If you are not married to the person, but in a non-related relationship (boyfriend, girlfriend, fiancé(e), or even just a friend), I would highly recommend (and I cannot say this strongly enough) give great consideration to walking away and not looking back. That being said, if you have a strong relationship with God and you know without any doubt that you are supposed to be connected to that person (and I really mean without a doubt!), maybe spend a little more time in prayer just to gain absolute confirmation, because God loves you so much and does not want to see His sons and daughters treated violently by anyone.

So, what kinds of things can you say or do to help move a person with NPD toward progress? Well, let's differentiate between what to say and what *not* to say.

Narcissists feel attacked very easily—likely because they attack others so easily.

As I mentioned earlier, straight from the mouth of a narcissist, "when they feel attacked, they feel they need to attack," so it's kind of a cycle within the bigger cycle.

As you are going through the process of engaging with a narcissist, you will not always see the progress you want. If you are working through the cycles and making good use of the Learning Phase, sometimes you may see small glimpses of hope, sometimes you may see nothing at all, and sometimes you may get to see small breakthroughs. Every once in awhile you may make a significant breakthrough with the person; it's these breakthroughs that move the needle. When ground is gained during a breakthrough, it reframes the narcissist's mental framework. It's important to understand, however, that just because a breakthrough happens does not mean you have a full victory. The process is long and hard.

To share a little bit about my personal experience, after about three years of engaging the cycle with the person who had NPD, I came to a point where I felt absolutely hopeless. And this is coming from someone who understood the cycle and was seeing periodic breakthroughs. I didn't feel hopeless because I wasn't seeing progress . . . I felt hopeless because I felt as though no matter what progress was made, remaining connected with that person would always be my attempting to care for someone who would never truly value me back. I had known this person quite a bit longer than the three years of engaging the cycle and had been experiencing the narcissistic attacks throughout. Prior to engaging the learning cycles, no progress had been made.

Once I began to engage the cycles, notable progress was made, and I could honestly say that each year was getting better and better. But better was not enough. Around the time I began to feel hopeless I started having dreams; these went on for several nights in a row. In my dreams, I was walking away; I was building relationships with people who were kind and caring. A few days after these dreams, I was with the narcissist after this person had just come out of a dark cycle phase. This meant that the person was in the Learning Phase. The person asked if everything was okay, to which I responded saying I was "fine."

But inside, I was not okay. Of course, there were plenty of days when I was okay, and plenty of days when I was not okay, which was to be expected when dealing with this ongoing process—but this was anew level of *not okay*. This was a level of feeling internally hopeless and being ready to just walk away.

I decided to go ahead and share my dreams. I didn't go into detail, but simply said, "I want to tell you about my dreams; the dreams I've been having lately. For the last few nights, I've had dreams of just walking away, of throwing in the towel on trying to work out the relationship between you and me. I've had dreams about you being two different people; one that went on how you are now, and one that spent time with me and was kind and caring. I've had dreams about walking away from you and spending my time with people who actually value me as a person."

I then continued with, "Now, I'm not telling you that I am going to do these things, but I am telling you what's in my subconscious. I can't control my dreams, and they are displaying what I'm feeling."

I paused for a moment and then followed that up with another attempt to set boundaries. "I will tell you that the things you say and the names you call me that degrade me are not welcome and they are not okay."

Surprisingly, and unbeknownst to me, we were on the verge of another breakthrough. Just a few hours later we had a couple of conversations: one about simple tasks, another about conversation context, and another about expectations.

In those conversations, the person with NPD brought up how the feeling of being attacked and accused had arisen during a simple question on a previous day.

This was a door to advance the progress. I was surprised by how far it went. After discussing the feeling of accusation, I walked through how my question had simply been a question, and the sense of attack had been an internalized misunderstanding, whereby the narcissist had turned the question into an accusation where no intention of accusation had actually existed.

The person actually opened up and allowed this understanding to sink in. I asked if this person could stop to evaluate whether the accusation perceived may not have been an accusation the next time it's interpreted. In response, the narcissist made a request of me.

The person asked if I could be sensitive with my tone, to make the delivery of my questions sound more kind. This was a serious request for me. I'd been on guard for so long, with my walls up, that I indeed had lost quite a bit of my kindness in tone. I had the kindness for most other people, just not with this person. It wasn't that I sounded rude or mean, I was simply flat or joyless in tone. If the person with NPD was truly going to take steps, I was going to try as well.

Over the next couple days, I applied intentional kindness in my tone. The other person exhibited actions of caring that were uncommon—communicating when plans changed (instead of standing me up), and other courteous types of actions.

I've been a rare observer of someone's making progress with narcissism. While it is not easy, it can happen. Consistent and intentional work needs to be put in by someone who is not the narcissist in order for progress to be made, but it is possible.

Even as Growth Takes Place . . .

Seeing growth can bring great hope, but it is not the end of the process. Telling the person with NPD that he or she didn't do something quite correctly or that it wasn't complete or to the extent that was needed—even after growth—is a trigger for an attack. And such a statement, even if cautiously worded, is interpreted by the person with NPD as an attack against his or her character or abilities, and that person is bound to turn it back on you and roll out some level of counterattack, even though the original statement may very well have been simple and well-meaning in nature.

Sometimes making such statements is necessary—but just be aware of the response that verbalizing those statements will incur.

These discussions can productively take place (to an extent) if during a Learning Phase of the cycle.

That is the phase where all progress is made.

Why do I attract Narcissists

Chapter 6

If you have been in relationships with more than one narcissist, you may begin to wonder if you just attract narcissists. If this isn't applicable to you, then this chapter may not apply—but it may still help to provide some insight for you both in how you view your relationship with the narcissist, and how the narcissist tends to become attracted to people.

Let's talk a little about the narcissist first, and then we'll dive into why we may find ourselves in relationships with people who have narcissistic personality disorders, or narcissistic personality traits.

So first, what does a narcissist look for in their targets that attracts them? Well, independence is a big one. This is not simply the ability to be a capable person, but someone who sees himself or herself as truly "independent." Oftentimes this is accompanied by the inability for one to fully connect with his or her own needs and, possibly, even his or her own true feelings. This "independence" and perceived non-need for the help of others seems to be a challenge to narcissists to see if they can “break” the independent person.

Independence with self-guilt is another element that can attract a narcissist. The independent part draws from the same as the above, but the “self-guilt” portion—where someone hasn't truly forgiven him-or herself for a past mistake or circumstance—that part gives the narcissist ammunition to start with, a vulnerability to exploit early on . . . something to tuck away for a future attack.

But there is also the question of, why do people accept narcissists or keep them?

One reference suggests that they "are very good at creating a fantastical, flattering self-image that draws us in" (Smith, M. & Robinson, L.). In addition, people who accept a relationship with a narcissist may have turned down previous relationships with others because the previous person seemed "too nice." When they then consider a relationship with the person with NPD, this is a person who has some "not so nice" characteristics—they just don't know to what extent they are signing up for it.

Once they are in, they feel committed to the decision to agree to the relationship. Walking away once the narcissist's true character is revealed feels like "quitting," and these independent people rarely allow themselves to succumb to quitting. They create a belief that they can overcome this.

Using these tactics, maybe you can, but it will take a lot of energy—energy that could be much better used on positive and productive life activities.

You may be the glass-half-full type of person, always looking for the best in people. You may have tended to put more focus on the narcissistic person during those light times, while thinking or hoping that those dark times are just moments in time that will pass. There's a hoping-for-the-best mentality that those types of actions and behaviors were just the results of a "bad day," without understanding that it is a continuous cycle for people with NPD. Narcissistic Personality Disorder is also not widely understood by the general public, so many people don't even know what signs to interpret as potential symptoms of NPD. I suspect that many people don't know they are dealing with a personality disorder until they are deep into that relationship and they either look up the symptoms or talk to someone who recognizes them.

Ultimately, people have healthy and unhealthy characteristics. Not all unhealthy characteristics look dangerous, but these can have unhealthy effects. Looking back, I see that early on in that relationship, I had been uncomfortable with emotion, generally speaking, being far more comfortable with facts and logic. I did not connect to my own emotions well, and thus I was more susceptible to allowing a person into my life who also could not connect with my emotions. Had I been aware of this in those early years, I may have been able to see that as a red flag.

There is a great book on healthy versus unhealthy people and what this looks like; it is called *Safe People,* by Dr. Henry Cloud and Dr. John Townsend. It provides valuable insight introspectively to the reader as well as outwardly in recognizing these traits and characteristics in others.

For potential romantic or spousal relationships, there are some things to be aware of in order to avoid attracting those with NPD in the future. From personal experience, I would recommend learning a little more about yourself and being comfortable with your own emotions.

A good step here that can help is to begin to intentionally incorporate "feelings words" into your everyday communication when you notice an emotion either in yourself or others. The difference between not acknowledging the feeling and acknowledging it could be simple. It may look something like, "it made me feel good when . . ." versus "it made me feel happy when . . . ." In the first, the word "good" is a descriptor, but is not a "feelings" word. The second example uses the word "happy," which is a feelings word. The simple act of using feelings words can be an open door to your becoming more comfortable with your own feelings and the feelings of others. If connecting with your feelings is not a problem for you, then another good self-discovery is understanding what your boundaries and expectations are for relational engagement. Once you have a solid understanding of what you are willing and not willing to accept, stick by that. Also, surround yourself with a few friends that can help hold you accountable to your expectations and boundaries.

Here's another link to an article in *Psychology Today* that may be helpful as you think about what you are no longer willing to accept or tolerate and help you think about where boundaries should be set.

https://www.psychologytoday.com/us/blog/understanding-narcissism/201708/why-do-narcissists-abuse-those-they-love).

In some cases, you didn't choose them or invite them into your life—you may have one as a relative, such as a parent, sibling, or child. In those cases, you are still able to set boundaries, and you are still under no obligation to hold that person as an actively engaged part of your daily life.

There are different support groups out there. Many people have walked through the path you are walking. Reach out; conduct a search. Connect with others who have already discovered ways to overcome and relate. Remember that you are not meant to do life alone. Build a network of people around you whom you can learn from, and with whom you can talk and be accountable. These could be people inside and outside the groups in your everyday life. There are so many resources at our fingertips now. People are often willing to listen, help, and/or connect. All you need to do is ask. While not everyone is able, don't take a "no" personally—ask someone else or find a forum. You are not alone. This struggle with people who have NPD is far more common than I wish it were.

Ultimately

Chapter 7

Ultimately, not every ending is a happy ending. Ultimately, you can't make somebody change. Ultimately, the efforts you put forth—even if they're the right ones that can bring change—may not make enough of a difference, and those actions taken by the narcissistic person may ultimately be too much to have a story of coming out of narcissism.

People with narcissism are masters of deception. They go so much into their own lies and deception that it becomes such a tightly woven fabric that I'm not even sure if they themselves can clearly identify where reality ends and the lies begin. You could say they live in a different reality (or, rather, sub-reality), from everyone else—a sub-reality that revolves around their own distortions . . . a fictitious world into which they would like to bring others to dwell with them.

If You Choose to Disconnect

If you do choose to sever the relationship with the person with NPD, or even just remove yourself from relational contact by a degree or two, it won't be without challenges.

Persons with narcissism won't give up their perceived grasp easily. They can't stand losing control and will try multiple approaches to regain the position of power when they sense their target is pulling away.

You can expect the following tactics—and just like former attack approaches, they may be recycled, trying each again and again in multiple forms within their limited arsenal.

1. They will guilt you (aiming at others or themselves, trying to paint a picture that you are ruining or hurting the well-being of others through the separation).

2. They will make grand gestures (offering gifts, promises of future paradise or appealing plans).

3. They will twist past events (as they did within the relationship). (They are masters of deception, and will twist past events, particularly those of their own poor actions, striving to convince you that you are overreacting and it wasn't as bad as you are making it out to be. They may even admit what they did if you recount it, but then a couple sentences later will discount the very thing he or she just admitted. They will work to make you doubt what you know of your own reality, memory, and sanity.)

4. They will play the victim (their world revolves around them). (When they sense they are losing control, they will often play the victim to arouse sympathy for their distorted cause. This could be in the form of the "pain" they are feeling, that they can't be successful or fulfill their dreams without you, or even how they "can't live without you.")

5. They will turn the tables (they may twist the scene and try to convince you that you wronged them, or that it's your fault).

6. They will impose jealousy tactics (they may do or say things to try to make you jealous or feel that you are missing out by not being with them).

7. They will incorporate smear tactics or alliance building. (They may try to publicly make you look bad in an attempt to gain public option control over you. Or they may go to those in your relationship web with an attempt to gather them on their side, seeing you as the villain or the one at fault. They may even attempt to rally others to contact you to convince you to reconsider and oblige the narcissist's cause.

8. They may barrage you (they may incessantly call you, message you, or otherwise try to regain communication through which they can apply their tactics).

9. They may use the silent treatment. (This may come as a tactic that mixes many of the others. If after barraging you does not return their desired result, they may

cut all communication. While this may sound like a relief—and it is—it may be an attempt to ignite jealousy or sympathy that you suddenly stopped hearing from them. Resist any urge to follow up and take it as the blessing it is.)

10. They will project. (Just as was a common behavior throughout the relationship, they may continue to try to project their behavior onto you.)

11. They will show a lack of boundaries (they don't suddenly respect your boundaries after cutting off or backing away from a relationship with a narcissist). (They may pop up unannounced, try to contact you incessantly, and otherwise ignore any and all boundaries. You must continue to reinforce your boundaries even after exiting or minimizing the relationship.)

The ways of a person with NPD don't adhere to the same standards or expectations as most other people. While retreating from a relationship with a friend, family member, or romantic partner can be a difficult thing to do in any scenario, one such as with a narcissist person isa fully engaging process.

You can expect at least a year, if not more, of intentional countermeasures as you take a stand and wield your shield against distortion, deception, and common tactics of a narcissist who is attempting to lure, coerce, or otherwise position you back into his or her domain.

If You Choose to Push Through

This is not a battle for the strong or for the weak. This is a battle that you must walk with the Lord through Christ Jesus, because when He defines you, that's when you can never become lost. You may feel darkness come on and the pain may be intense, but the words that come as arrows from all around will not define you. The word that God speaks defines who you are—that you are loved, that you are precious in His sight, that you are chosen by Him, that you are beautiful, and that you are cherished. These are the things that will define me, and when you know yourself through the eyes of Christ, these are the things that will define you.

However your story ends, may you be defined through the eyes of One who knows you . . . who truly sees you. I pray that your story has a happy ending.

Bibliography

A recommended listen is the song "The Father's House" by CoryAsbury.

Bibliography

Cloud, H., and J. Townsend. *Safe People: How to Find Relationships That Are Good for You and Avoid Those That Aren't.* Grand Rapids, MI: Zondervan, 1995.

"Diseases & Conditions: Narcissistic Personality Disorder," Mayo Clinic. https://www.mayoclinic.org/diseases-conditions/narcissistic-p ersonality disorder/symptoms-causes/syc-20366662(accessed May 2019). *The site seems to have been updated since the time of the initial identification and may not reflect the same content or language.*

French, Mandy. "Projection in Psychology Explained." *Medical News Today,* August 1, 2023.

https://www.medicalnewstoday.com/articles/projection-in-psychology#:~:text=Summary,help%20stop%20and%20prevent%20projection(accessed October 25, 2024).

Greenburg, Elinor, PhD. "Why Do Narcissists Abuse Those They Love?" *Psychology Today*, August 4, 2017. https://www.psychologytoday.com/us/blog/understanding-narcissism/201708/why-do-narcissists-abuse-those-they-love(accessed April 5, 2024).

Greenburg, Melanie, PhD. "Are Narcissists Actually Covering Up Insecurity?" *PsychologyToday*, March 29, 2021. https://www.psychologytoday.com/us/blog/the-mindful-self-express/202103/are-narcissists-actually-covering-up-insecurity(accessed August 16, 2024).

Restivo, Jenette. Harvard Health Publishing. "Narcissistic personality disorder: Symptoms, diagnosis, and treatments." Harvard Health Publishing, January 8, 2024. https://www.health.harvard.edu/mind-and-mood/narcissistic-personality-disorder-symptoms-diagnosis-and-treatments (accessed April 2, 2025).

Smith, Melinda, M.A., and Lawrence Robinson. "Narcissistic Personality Disorder (NPD)." HelpGuide.org, updated March 13, 2025. https://www.helpguide.org/articles/mental-disorders/narcissistic-personality-disorder.htm.

About the author

Jessie Lee Perez is bridging the gap of processes and relationships in ways that are truly transforming lives. As successful author, coach, businesswoman and the founder of We Speak Color Inc., she is widely known for expertise in the area of the human temperament and for her incredible book Color By Design. The book is entertaining and written for the everyday person, yet based on fundamental scientific and psychological principles of the human design that Jessie uses to help us understand ourselves and those around us, leading to transformation, reconciliation and growth both in our personal and professional lives.

Jessie is a faith-filled woman, holds a degree from Regent University and has extensive international experience, having worked or served in 18 nations. As an IIBA Certified Business Analyst, she leverages her wealth of business practice experience combined with her expertise in the human temperament arena to create a truly remarkable and unique offering that is easy to apply.

Above all she wants to help everyone see that "Together We Are More".

Also by

Additional books by Jessie Lee Perez include:

Color By Design: Why You Do What You Do, Think What You Think, and Care about What You Care About

(also available in additional languages)

The Ways of a Business Analyst

www.ingramcontent.com/pod-product-compliance
Lightning Source LLC
LaVergne TN
LVHW100325210926
848480LV00003B/1255